MASONIC HALLS OF ENGLAND

The Midlands

The Halls covered in other volumes in this series are:

The SOUTH

Barnstaple
Bath
Bradford-on-Avon
Brighton
Bristol
Canterbury
Cheltenham
Exeter
Faversham
Jersey
Langport
Lewes
Liskeard
Newport (IoW)
Poole
St Austell
Taunton
Torbay
Weymouth
Windsor

The NORTH

Alnwick
Barton-upon-Humber
Berwick
Beverley
Bolton
Bradford
Carlisle
Durham
Huddersfield
Kingston-upon-Hull
Liverpool
Manchester
Newcastle-upon-Tyne
Sunderland
Wakefield
Warrington
Whitby
Whitehaven
York
Halifax

Opposite: *Guy's Cliff, Warwick.*

MASONIC HALLS OF ENGLAND

THE MIDLANDS

The Revd Neville Barker Cryer

LEWIS MASONIC

IAN ALLAN GROUP

In the same series

Masonic Halls of England—The South

Masonic Halls of England—The North

© 1989
N. B. Cryer

Published by Lewis Masonic
IAN ALLAN REGALIA LTD, Terminal House, Shepperton
who are members of the
IAN ALLAN GROUP

First published in England in 1989

British Library Cataloguing in Publication Data
Cryer, Neville B.
  Masonic halls of England.
  The Midlands
  1. England. Freemasons. Lodge. Halls
  I. Title
  942

ISBN 0 85318 164 0

Printed in Great Britain by
Latimer Trend & Company Ltd, Plymouth

CONTENTS

FOREWORD

FOR MORE than a century Masonic historians have been concerned in researching the origins and development of the Craft. Little, however, appears to have been done in recording the most publicly visible evidence of our existence: the places where we meet. From my own experience of visiting lodges in England and Wales I know the great wealth of history and variation in style evidenced by the many Halls and Lodge Rooms used by our lodges. The Rev. Neville Barker Cryer is to be congratulated both for bringing this aspect of our history to our attention and for recording it now for those who will follow us in years to come.

M. B. S. Higham
Commander, R.N.
Grand Secretary.

PREFACE

THE WRITING OF this book, like the other volumes in this series, has given the author a great deal of pleasure. It has permitted me to appreciate something of the breadth and depth of English Freemasonry at the present time as well as allowing me the delight of seeing the wealth of treasures which we still possess and of meeting some of the dedicated masons who have undertaken to preserve for the future those heirlooms they have received from the past.

It has been a journey of constant surprises as door after door has been opened to reveal the temple interiors and their contents, sometimes in almost the same manner as they were first seen 150 or 100 years ago. It is the joy of that discovery, and the interest aroused in seeing so many items of peculiar fascination for the masonic student that led me to believe that we should produce this and the other volumes.

My first concern therefore has been to record for the present generation and for posterity something of what the Craft has handed down to us from its very beginnings in this land. Many, I believe, will, like myself, be pleasantly surprised by the variety and richness of the different halls which are illustrated here, whether it be the parish church conversions of Colchester and Shrewsbury, the palatial suites of Birmingham, the Egyptian symbolism of Boston or the mediaeval setting of Warwick. Every location has its own fascination especially when, as I hope I have shown, the building also contains particular treasures that are known nowhere else or only rarely so. I hope that this survey of intriguing halls in the Midlands will raise the spirits of masons at this time and make them quietly proud of the heritage that is theirs.

The second purpose of my writing has been to try and encourage a greater diligence throughout our land in looking at and understanding the possessions in freemasonry that we may have in our own locality. It has been my experience that my visit to a temple or its museum has often renewed interest in its contents for the masons who regularly and normally meet there. Too many of us are not aware of the treasure trove that lies around us and there is all the more danger that if this unconscious indifference is not stemmed there could be examples of the kind of loss of previous pieces of the past such as have already occurred in some centres. If you ask some masons in a place that has a long tradition where are their old tracing boards, chapter banners, globes or pillars the answer is either 'we don't know' or 'Ah! now we do have some stacked somewhere'. Once the items are unearthed and explained, there is a new sense of pride awakened and a determination to look after these heirlooms with more care.

Thirdly, I wanted to encourage masons who travel around the country to go and see some of the halls and their contents that are mentioned here. It has long been a custom for people on their holidays to enter an old parish church, a castle or manor house and wonder at the relics of the past of our nation. Here, for freemasons, is the beginning of a guide for some of our peculiar heritage in English history. I hope sincerely that readers will take this book with them on their journeys and ring up the local Provincial or lodge secretary and ask whether a visit to these halls is possible. It will well repay you to see these halls for yourself.

As I have travelled around this land and responded to the information about interesting halls that has been provided for me I have been only too well aware that I may be overlooking some gems of masonic interest that I ought to have included here. Despite the fact that there will be at least two volumes in the series with this one—covering the North of England and the South—I am sure that there will be some who will want to draw my attention to treasures overlooked. With the encouragement of the publisher I invite anyone who would wish to do so to write to me at Shepperton and give me details of their hall and its contents. I am sure that future editions of this volume or others in the series can benefit from being kept as comprehensive as possible. It may even be that we shall find ourselves with enough material for yet another volume in the series. It will be good to know that this book has stimulated such interest in *Masonic Halls of England*.

The Revd Neville Barker Cryer
1988

ACKNOWLEDGEMENTS

NO BOOK SUCH as this could possibly have been completed without the help of a large number of collaborators. I shall attempt to name many of these below but it would be impossible to mention the countless Provincial Grand Masters, Provincial Secretaries and their staffs who have assisted me with suggestions, contacts, directions for travel, and in some cases actual hospitality. I am deeply grateful to them all and I want to state here that had it not been for them and their work then this book would not even have been possible, and certainly not in the time available.

Having been put in touch with individual halls, and the lodges associated with them, I specially want to thank the following for their interest before, during and following my visits and for being willing in each case to check the script of my chapter for their hall so that it is as accurate as possible. Any remaining errors must still be laid at my door.

(Birmingham) D.C. Hobson, W. Rogers; (Boston) L. Ringrose; (Colchester) A.E. Bayne, A. Garner; (Ipswich) E.H. Hanson; (King's Lynn) D. Woolnough; (Knutsford) S. Tracey; (Leicester) C.C Stoop, L.E. Hutchinson; (Letchworth) E. Nicholls; (Ludlow) C. Francis; (Norwich) A.W. Aliffe; (Shrewsbury) C.H.D. Done; (Spilsby) R. Cooke-Barnes; (Stamford) O.N.N. Hart, T.C. Fahie, J. Linnell; (Stony Stratford) N. Walton; (Warwick) D. Palmer, P.F. Porter; (Worksop) R. Jackson; (Great Yarmouth) J.G. Duffield, A.W. Aliffe. Thanks are also due to John Hamill, Librarian and Curator of the United Grand Lodge of England library and museum for assisting in the supply of illustrations. To numerous photographers who have supplied illustrations, some anonymously, and to all of these brethren, as well as many others whose names I have not recalled I extend the very warmest of thanks and express my delight at making so many more masonic friends.

1 Birmingham
2 Boston
3 Colchester
4 Ipswich
5 King's Lynn
6 Knutsford
7 Leicester
8 Letchworth
9 Ludlow
10 Norwich
11 Nottingham
12 Peterborough
13 Shrewsbury
14 Spilsby
15 Stamford
16 Stony Stratford
17 Warwick
18 Worksop
19 Great Yarmouth

BIRMINGHAM

The Masonic Hall in Clarendon Road

EDGBASTON HAS ALWAYS been a most distinctive part of the city of Birmingham. Its many tree-lined streets and avenues, its large Victorian detached houses, its reputation as an important centre for English cricket, the presence still of the Oratory buildings for ever associated with Cardinal John Henry Newman, and the lingering awareness that this was the home and political stamping ground of the Chamberlains—all combine to make this area one of historical fascination. It may now be a vast thoroughfare for traffic to the north and west, its large dwellings either business premises or the core of new hotels, but still it retains a character and place in the capital of the Midlands. It is a fitting place for the masonic centre of Warwickshire.

A demonstration of mid-eighteenth century masonic practice as given by the Sutton Coldfield Masonic Study Circle shows how natural it was for lodges in Birmingham, as in so many others visited in this book, to occupy taverns and inns where a convenient room could be found for the lodge itself to assemble in some kind of privacy. Indeed the very first lodge to be formed in the city, now St Paul's Lodge No 43, met at no fewer than 12 locations (albeit one of them twice in 30 years) between the years 1733 and 1869. The next lodge, No 149, when it was constituted in 1736, started its meeting at the King's Arms, Edgbaston Street in 1736, moved to the St George and Dragon in Digbeth in 1739, back to the Rose, also in Edgbaston Street, and then moved to Wolverhampton in 1766 before being erased in 1772. St Alban's, Union, St John's, (later to become one of Warwickshire's 'Shakespeare' lodges) and Athol Lodges followed much the same, if less lengthy, pattern of moving from tavern to tavern and though the first three of these were erased, Athol, now 74, had four homes in hostelries before taking over the Synagogue in Severn Street and making that into a Masonic Hall. It is worth recording that since that purchase in 1858 the building has been in continuous masonic occupation and is the longest serving Masonic Hall in the Province. It is also worth noting that in 1864 the Deputy Provincial Grand Master, WBro Elkington, visited the Athol Lodge to explain that plans were now in hand to purchase all the properties belonging to the local lodges so that the proceeds might be amalgamated and enable a new Masonic Hall to be erected in New Street. The Athol lodge brethren were not impressed by the idea and at a subsequent meeting decided, on the contrary, to add a banqueting hall to their satisfactory accommodation. In 1970/71 it was even further modernised.

Howe Lodge, No 587, was the first lodge to set a new trend in not meeting on licensed premises. It was originally a non-dining lodge and met in rooms over the

Old Coal Wharf, Newhall Street. In 1855 the lodge took the lease of a house at the top end of the same street and by means of extensive alterations and the erection of a lodge room at the rear of the lodge became owners of 'the most commodious premises for Masonic purposes in the Province of Warwickshire'. By 1863 there were 14 lodges and chapters meeting in these rooms.

Generally, however, complaints were being heard more frequently in the 1860s about the inconvenience and bad ventilation at Newhall Street. Bro Elkington, not surprisingly, took the chair of a meeting to form a new limited liability company which would develop a piece of land in New Street, Birmingham. The capital was for £10,000 in 2000 shares at £5 each. 647 went on the occasion of the very first meeting date. The venture prospered and by 20 September, 1865 Lord Leigh had laid the foundation stone. In a most useful paper entitled 'The Masonic Meeting Places of Warwickshire' Bro Derrick C. Hobson has reproduced the following report from a contemporary Birmingham newspaper:

> The style of the building will be in conformity with the instructions to the architects, strictly classical, the exterior partaking rather of the Greek severity of treatment, while the interior will be carried out in a manner somewhat more free in character. The erections will comprise on the ground floor, the grand entrance in New Street, and shops similarly disposed to those in the Exchange Buildings by the same architect, with living rooms, etc. in the basement and warehouse in Pinfold Street. The remainder of the basement and sub-basement will be occupied by vaults and cellerage.

The Masonic temple at Edgbaston.

On the mezzanine storey will be the smaller lodge rooms, each 28 feet by 25 feet, with preparing-rooms, ante-rooms, regalia rooms, lobbies and monument rooms adjoining, and on the same floor the offices for the Secretary, and the club smoking room.

Ascending by a grand staircase on the first floor, and over the smaller masonic rooms, will be the grand banqueting hall, 71 feet 6 inches by 40 feet and 32 feet high. This hall will have a richly panelled and ornamented coved ceiling, springing from an entablature carried by marble columns with carved Corinthian capitals. A spacious 'orchestra' will form a prominent feature in the design of the room, and adjoining will be ante- and retiring rooms. The portion of the building on the first, second, and third floors facing New Street, will be set apart for the purposes of the club, with a separate staircase from the ground floor. These rooms will be decorated in every respect, worthy of a first class club. A very prominent feature in these rooms will be an angle-projecting window, a somewhat difficult subject to treat in a classical design.

The Grand Lodge Room, together with the other rooms necessary for the carrying on of the objects of the craft in a proper manner are to be on the third floor. The Grand Lodge Room will be similar in area to the grand banqueting hall, but four feet less in height, and will be lighted from the ceiling when required. The kitchens and servants' rooms will be placed at the top of the building and lifts will communicate with the various landings and serving rooms throughout. In addition, there are to be service stairs and several bedrooms and dressing rooms, and closets in every available corner (sic), and from an inspection of the plans we are enabled to say that none of the space at the disposal of the selected architect, Mr Edward Holmes, has been lost.

The main hall and museum.

The procession on the day was led by the Police and Regimental Band of the 1st Warwickshire Rifle Volunteers. At the site of the building the foundation stone was laid with full masonic ceremony, an anthem sung and oration delivered, with the National Anthem to close. At the banquet that followed the charge was 12s 6d for a gentleman, and 10s 6d for a lady, but one guinea for a double ticket!

I have retailed the details of this great event because it was important for the reader to appreciate that the building consecrated in 1870 at a Provincial Grand Lodge meeting under the banner of St Paul's Lodge was a very great acquisition for the Birmingham masons and was something that would need its equal or more when the time came to improve still further the local provision for masonic meetings. Indeed, as one reads the full account of what New Street looked like, it is possible to see how the best features there have been reproduced in the Clarendon Road suite at Edgbaston, 'toilets at every corner' excluded.

It was, in fact, to an interim temple that local masons moved on 23 September, 1927 The project had first been mooted in 1916 by Col Wyley, Deputy PGM, and it was in the form of a Warwickshire Peace Memorial that the Birmingham masons purchased the site in Broad Street in 1922. Another architectural competition was set up and 19 architects, who were all subscribing members of the Province, submitted designs. The prize was actually won by a PM of the Howe Lodge, No 587, WBro Rupert Savage. The need for the fresh provision is shown by the fact that despite the 16 craft lodges meeting in the old synagogue at Severn Street and 18 at New Street, not to mention the other degrees and orders, there were 12 Craft lodges meeting at the Imperial Hotel and two at the Grand Hotel. The creation of a new hall was therefore imperative and is to be noted that when the laying of the foundation stone took place it was by electrical remote control, thus giving to Sir Alfred Robbins, President of the Board of General Purposes, the idea for doing something similar at the stone-laying of the Great Queen Street site the following year. It was St Paul's Lodge that fittingly held the first meeting in the new hall in September 1927. Sadly, this hall, new as it was, did not provide the space that was really needed.

During the Second World War this temple was taken over by the government and was known locally as 'The Food Office'. Its occupation meant that a new masonic hall had to be found and fortunately the Edgbaston Assembly Rooms at the Five Ways became available. With the Provincial Grand Secretary's office sited at nearby Duchess Road these premises proved adequate until the present hall was opened.

Sir Stanley J. Harley, who was then the Provincial Grand Master, laid the foundation stone of the Clarendon Road Hall on 28 October, 1969, in what is now the kitchen area. It was transferred to what is now its more permanent and visible site at a later date. In doing so he expressed the hope that 'this place is not just an imposing, yet empty, shell but a power house of good influence and service to mankind in general'. It was a kind gesture that allowed the square to be applied to the stone by the Provincial Grand Master of the Mark Degree, and the level and plumbline by the Senior and Junior Grand Wardens respectively. It is also worth noting that the official brochure of the occasion speaks of this development being "the realisation of the dream that had occupied the minds of Warwickshire Masons since the inadequacy of our temporary meeting place in Francis Road was borne in upon us by the increasing strength of our order".

The building was completed in the autumn of 1971 and was duly dedicated by the Pro-Grand Master, the Rt Hon The Earl Cadogan, on 1 December at a meeting held again under the St Paul's Lodge banner. In this case the first body to hold a meeting there was the Warwickshire First Principals' Chapter no 4538 for the ceremony of installation. If in many of the halls visited and reported on in this volume the accent will be on antiquity and solid links with the past the emphasis here is nothing but modernity, efficiency and the sheer attractiveness of good design. All this, joined with ample space for parking, robing, movement and recreation. As a sample of what many future provincial centres could be, or may well be, like it is in itself memorable.

Some general statistics concerning this hall are in themselves impressive. $1\frac{1}{2}$ million bricks were used or as many as, laid end to end, would reach from Birmingham to Dover. The roof area is one acre, there are 600 doors, 2000 light fittings, seating for 2500 people at one time, 52 toilets, sufficient heating for 120 houses and enough electric cable to go to the top of Mount Everest and down the other side. The bricks, chosen especially for their mellow shade and enormous strength, came from a rural brickyard hidden in the depths of the Forest of Dean. Each brick was individually thrown by hand into a timber mould, a process unchanged from the days of ancient Babylon. Only the costs changed, with each brick here costing 30p for ordinary use, and some special ones mounting to £10 each. The basic framework was massive and is reminiscent of motorway bridge construction complete with civil engineering standard expansion and movement joints.

Portland stone was also introduced at various points to bring out special

The Grand Temple.

features. In this sense the load-bearing capacity of this material reflects the example set by Sir Christopher Wren and Inigo Jones, who first used it on any scale on their building of a new London. It may interest some readers to know that the care taken was such that while Shelly Whitbed was used for the pillars and columns, Roachbed was the stone chosen, for its character and texture, in the balcony fronts. The Roach is entirely made up of fossil casts.

The delightful and decorative timber used everywhere is specially selected black walnut. Great care has clearly been taken to ensure that the veneered panels were exactly matched and related to each other. This can best be seen and appreciated in the main dining room. To ensure the comfort of those both 'at labour' and 'at recreation' there are half a mile of ventilation grilles whilst 100,000 cubic feet of conditioned air is being moved every minute! The diners who can benefit from this provision are 350 in the one main room alone.

It would be obviously impossible in this book to guide a visitor to every part of the Warwickshire Masonic Temple but there are four areas that should be reported on here and are worth seeing by anyone who is able to visit this hall. The first is the museum. It is reached through the hotel-style vestibule, off which the Provincial Grand Secretary's office lies together with its boardroom. From here we pass a commodious buffet and luncheon bar into a second vestibule and turn right into the main hall. It is this lofty and spacious area with its many glass cases in the centre, and display boards round the sides, that houses the museum. Lit by natural light from a central fanlight during the day it is no less gently lit in the evening, and each of the display areas has its own special illumination.

Here we find specimens of glass and masonic emblems dating back over two centuries and more of our Craft history. Colourful banners adorn the upper balustrades, including one of that St Paul's Lodge when it was replaced in 1970. The cases show Staffordshire printed pink lustre ware, many unusual jewels and an array of old Verge watch movements with masonic emblems on their dials. There are some Delft punch bowls such as many a Tyler must have used to mix his 'special' in for a tavern meeting and alongside these are snuff boxes and masonically inscribed spoons. There are firing glasses with coloured, twisted stems which show that they are at least post-1850, and two very rare pieces, a large ruby loving-cup goblet which belonged to lodge of Integrity No 163 (then called Lodge of Industry), and a fine celery vase with a *mille fiore* base. This, like many other items, was the product of nearby Stourbridge.

There is a German rummer with a hollow stem which dates from c1625, and a large oval rummer of English design from about 1780. The jugs are a special feature in this collection—from Lowestoft, Liverpool, Leeds, as well as Staffordshire and there is a charming Worcestershire 'Etruscan Lodge' mug. One Sunderland ware jug here has a capacity of one gallon!

Amongst the examples of needlework are many pre-Union aprons of both English and French provenance. There are two excellent examples of hand-painted lambskin aprons and a magnificent early apron and collar of the Rose Croix. Scottish lodges are here well represented by clothing whilst at the head of the stairs leading from the museum there are two valuable Provincial swords. This is but a rapid survey of what would take much more space to describe to do it full justice and here, as in the library to follow, is more than enough material for masonic study.

On this floor one can easily reach the other lodge rooms, of which one is specially arranged for the Royal Arch and another for the Mark. It is to the library off this area that we have to move from here (as we found in Leicester, see Vol 2 and Manchester, Vol 3), where is a veritable treasure trove of manuscripts and books on a wide range of masonic and related subjects. Just a few of the collection's best pieces must be mentioned. There are copies of every edition of the Books of Constitutions from the first of the Premier Grand Lodge in 1723 up to the Union in 1813. Of the Engraved Lists there are editions from 1728 (the only known copy), 1737 (rare) and 1769 (very rare). There is an edition of Cole's Constitutions for 1728, a Breeches Bible (and it is always of masonic interest to know if the substitution of 'aprons' for 'breeches' in later bible editions was an influence of seventeenth century brethren) and, of course, first editions of Dugdale's 'Antiquities of Warwickshire' and Plot's 'Natural History of Stafford-shire'. The library is, indeed, so discreetly placed that whilst its contents are properly protected they may also miss the full attention of brethren that they deserve. A visitor must not miss it.

After going to the library let us mount the steps just mentioned and pass through the ante-room into the Grand Temple. Like the main dining room there is accommodation here for 350 brethren and both the Provincial Chapter and Grand Mark lodge can assemble here comfortably. Here we will find some fine Master and Wardens' chairs belonging to the Shakespeare Lodge No 284, previously meeting in Warwick, whilst two remarkable Chippendale Wardens' chairs belong-ing to the 1733-founded St Paul's Lodge are temporarily on loan to the Grand Lodge museum in London but would normally have their location here. Whilst the temple has none of those remarkable wall-decorations that we have seen in so many other locations there is about this room a grandeur and quality which carries its own distinction. It is a remarkable place in which to speak, as the author can well testify, and it more than amply meets the requirements of the large and impressive gatherings that assemble there.

Finally, here, we must not overlook the Clarendon Suite with its own separate and distinct entrance from Stirling Road, as well as internal access from the main dining room of the hall. There is here a grand ballroom with a specially-lit dancing floor, an excellent bar and the natural use of the adjoining large dining area without impinging on parallel masonic functions. Here is the perfect arrangement for involving families, ladies, and the general public without trespassing on those parts of the building that are 'peculiar' to brethren.

In the light of all these facilities and the evident links with the past, even in what at first sight may seem a Masonic Hall for the twentyfirst century, it can hardly be a surprise for the writers of the hall brochure to say, 'The brethren of Warwick-shire are immensely proud of their Temple and the Clarendon Suite—we cannot but feel that our visitors will be greatly impressed also'. Of that there can be little doubt. It is the kind of hall that one will long remember—and want to visit again.

BOSTON

The Masonic Hall with the Egyptian Porch

MANY PEOPLE WILL be familiar with the famous landmark called the Boston Stump. This 200-ft high tower of the Parish Church of St Botolph stands out with dramatic effect over what was originally called St Botolph's town and amidst the flat agricultural land around. It is a sight that can hardly be missed.

There will also be many masons who will have visited the Masonic Hall at Main Ridge in the same town though that is hardly likely to catch the eye in anything like the same manner. It is, however, one of the halls that has a character and history all of its own and in terms of Lincolnshire masonry it has a high claim to being one of their memorable temples. It is certainly a hall that leaves you in no doubt as to its uniqueness once you turn the corner of the street in which it stands.

There, on the edge of a perfectly normal English pavement, in the side street of an historic East Coast port, stands a portico which is pure Egyptian—the reproduction of the Temple of Dandour in Nubia. On either side of the entrance are two massive cylindrical pillars. The base is adorned with strong V-shaped decoration and the chapiters with the leaves and the fruit of the palm tree. Above this spreading carved foliage are two square blocks of stone bearing a huge stone lintel, which, like the blocks, is covered with Egyptian hieroglyphs. All this is then surrounded by a brick frame leading to an outward-curving cornice, decorated with a double-winged sphere at the centre itself half-encircled by, and resting upon, two contorted asps.

This same form of decoration adorns the massive square stone doorway between the pillars. The sphere here has three wings and on the lintel are carved Greek letters "ΓΝΩΘΙ ΣΕΑΥΤΟΝ" meaning 'Know Thyself'. Taken together, the Greek phrase and the sphere, the snake and the spreading wings, have a message that any studious craftsman in our speculative Art could discern. What is clear is that they were not mere decoration. This is proved by the fact that all the Egyptian writing was directed by Bro Cabourn Pocklington, who was intending to convey the following news to the informed Egyptologist freemason:

> In the 22nd year of the reign of Her Majesty, the Royal Daughter, Victoria, Lady most gracious, this Hall was erected; May it be prosperous:
> Zetland was Ruler of the Mysteries and St Albans Ruler of the District when this building was dedicated to the God of Truth, who lives for ever, in the year 1863, 5th month and 28th day.

Left: *The porchway or entrance, Boston.*

The Lodge of Harmony, the sole occupant of the hall at that time, was then in its 57th year. Its warrant shows the date of 20 August, 1789 but this was for a former lodge that was authorized to meet at the White Hart in the Drapery, Northampton. By 1792 no returns were being made and those who still belonged to that body sought to recoup their losses by disposing of their warrant to Boston brethren who in 1805 are recorded as having been initiated in the Witham Lodge at Lincoln. The previous warrant is therefore endorsed with the words—'on application of the brethren of the said lodge and with the approbation of the Deputy Grand Master Admiral Sir Peter Parker Baronet it was removed to the Ship Tavern in the Borough of Boston in the County of Lincoln to be there held under the aforesaid name (of Harmony)' Signed by Wm White, GS 18 January AL 5806 AD 1806.

The lodge here took off at a fair rate. On 4 February, 1806 the brethren settled their subscription rate, proposed 7 candidates and agreed a warm vote of thanks 'in consideration of the marked attention shewn by (Bro Whitwell) for the welfare of this lodge'. Bro Whitwell belonged to St Peter's Lodge in Peterborough and he had been the one responsible for enabling the Boston masons to secure the Northampton warrant. By 1812 the number of initiations had risen to 29 and there were 70 members on the roll.

One of the unique items connected with this start of the new lodge is the first apron as worn at the consecration of the 'new' Lodge of Harmony in Boston. The apron was of lamb skin, 20 in deep by 15 in broad and with a semi-circular flap of 8 in radius. There were no tassels but a very dark blue ribbon edging, even on the flap. The apron was not lined and the strings to tie it were simply the continuation of the ribbon edging.

The main design of the apron consists of a platform of three steps all chequered. In the centre at the foot is an arch over water and on this an ark is floating, whilst above the ark a dove with an olive branch is in flight. Above the arch is an altar with the Bible opened at the second book of Chronicles, chapters 2 and 3 (where Solomon determines to build the Temple and two Hirams come to assist him) and behind the Bible is a rising sun with an all-seeing eye.

Also on the platform are 3 lights, the rough and perfect ashlars with a tracing board showing the 47th Proposition. At the ends of the platform are two pedestals with the figures of Hope on the left and Faith on the right. One also sees embroidered a ladder above with FH and C upon its staves, the circle and parallels with a glory below; a sword and key, a square, a level and a plumbline. Charity appears on the flap as a woman attending to children and in the two corners to each side are the moon and seven stars. The date on the apron is 14 February, 1803, suggesting that this design was submitted for approval and use when the lodge was ready to buy and use such aprons. It can certainly be seen what a colourful and meaningful thing it was for brethren to be clothed. Tracing boards were less a necessity.

As early as 1809 the inconvenience and objections to holding the lodge in the surroundings of an inn were already being felt. There was even a motion, strange to us, that the lodge 'be held in a private room'. That does not seem to have had much effect for it is noted that in 1819 they removed to premises in Church Street belonging to a Bro Tuxford, a solicitor, to achieve that object.

At the present time when some would seem to warn the public about the deleterious effects of the Craft it would be good if they could see another of the

The main temple looking east. Mounted on the wall above the Master's pedestal is the symbol from the Temple of Edfon.

present hall's possessions—a Ground Plan of Boston Church drawn 'from actual measurements' and dedicated to the Lodge of Harmony by a Mr William Brand, a resident of Boston. he wrote:

> In honourable testimony of the advantages possessed by the Public in the present era from the Fraternity of Freemasons, this Plan is respectfully inscribed to the Masters (*sic*), Wardens, Treasurer, Stewards and Brethren of the Lodge of Harmony . . . by their obedt. humble servant

Signed by Wm Brand, 2 March 1811. It is interesting that the Secretary is omitted.

Dissension and disaffection must have developed in the 1820s for the lodge closed between 1830 and 1833 and when 15 brethren met at the Dolphin Inn in the latter year it was 'for the revival of the Lodge from its dormant state'. It is not our purpose here to record the varying fortunes of the Lodge of Harmony save to remark that by the time the Jubilee arrived in 1856 the brethren who had left to form a new lodge of St Botolph had removed to Sleaford and the way was open for Bro Pocklington as WM to celebrate the occasion with a question and answer session on the first three sections of the lecture in the first degree. That was very appropriate for it was to be Bro Pocklington who was foremost in urging the committee in 1859 to consider adopting a style for the proposed new and private Masonic Hall in Main Ridge that would endorse the Lectures which teach that 'our usages and customs were derived from the Ancient Egyptians'.

In the thirties of the last century Main Ridge was a narrow street bounded on one side by an extensive area called 'Inlay's Garden'. Opposite was a paddock, belonging to a Mr Thirkill, which projected into the street and was adjoined by an open sewer called the Bar Ditch. This paddock was fenced with an old hawthorn hedge which was in a dilapidated state. A Mr Hopkins attacked the hedge and field projection, won a court case against it, and Mr Thirkill built the present wall, had the sewer arched over and the street was able to be widened to a further ten feet.

The present building is actually constructed on part of Inlay's Garden and was arranged by a committee in 1869 who recognised that what the then IPM had arranged (a banquet in the same room as the meeting) set the tone for the future and so there was need of a meeting place where there would be a temple, committee rooms and a dining area with a kitchen. Shares of £5 each were issued and 60 brethren took them up.

The building that resulted from the laying of the corner stone on 20 April, 1860 comprised an entrance hall, kitchen and banquet room on the ground floor (now since developed with a bar and lounge area), and a real winding stairway, albeit square and not circular, to the robing rooms, Tyler's area and temple proper above. This latter room, still the same as it was over 125 years ago, is 40 feet long and 20 feet broad. It is a perfect double cube, as might have been imagined with brethren like Pocklington and Clegg present at the time. They must have taken great pains to emphasise the similarities and symbolism of this structure as compared with the Egyptian temples of Edfon and Phile, as well as Solomon's Temple in Jerusalem.

The decoration of the temple took three years to complete and the results of that kind of attention—even though the brethren used the lodge room in the meantime—is now evident for all to see. It makes the interior as unusual as the entrance

Left top: *The symbol from the Temple of Edfon representing a triangle superimposed upon rays of light with the 'Master's Hand' holding a Cross.*

Bottom: *Immediately above the temple entrance is a reproduction of a scarabaeus or beetle whilst above that is a serpent encircling a winged world.*

Below: *The plaque above the Junior Warden's chair commemorating the Opening and Closing Odes written by Walter Clegg who was a member of Lodge of Harmony No 272 at Boston. The Odes are those frequently sung in lodges throughout the English constitution.*

and it is significant that the request for dedication by the R W Duke of St Albans, the Provincial Grand Master, was not made until everything was in order. He came on 28 May, 1863. For his, and the brethren's, edification Bro Clegg illustrated the various items in the lodge décor.

The symbol over the Master's chair is from the Temple of Edfon, representing a triangle superimposed upon rays of light with the 'Master's hand' holding a Cross in the centre, meaning the Key of Light and Knowledge, as in Habakkuk III, verse 4. (c.f. the 'hand' at Brighton in Vol. I)

The symbol in the north represents a lotus plant resting upon a triangle surrounded by an endless serpent, and rays of glory again emerging from the whole. The lotus plant suggests different stages of growth—infancy, youth, manhood and old age, whilst the serpent represents eternity.

The disc of the Sun with an equilateral triangle found on the ceiling symbolises the True God, 'Him that sitteth upon the circle of the earth' and is found everywhere on the ancient monuments of Egypt, as it is also frequently represented in mediaeval Christian imagery.

The scarabaeus or beetle is reproduced thrice over the doorway and is copied from such representations at Karnac on the upper Nile. It always covered their doorways and signifies Industry, Patience and Secrecy.

This same Bro Clegg has yet another claim to fame. As a plaque near the organ states it was WBro Walter Clegg MRCS, PPGW (Lincs.), Master of the Lodge of Harmony in 1859 who wrote the lyrics for 'Hail eternal', the ode which so many lodges use at the opening, and 'Now the evening shadows closing' for the closing of a lodge. The music was composed by Bro Walter B Gilbert, Mus Doc, in 1869. He was organist of the lodge. What is certain is that at the Dedication Festival of the Hall we have been looking at, and at the Lincolnshire Provincial Grand Lodge meeting held at the Assembly Rooms, Boston the same day, these odes were used at the appropriate points, though the Provincial Grand Organist, Bro Keller, must have devised other music for their accompaniment. The plaque recording the main facts above was itself dedicated and placed in position on 10 January, 1967.

As one looks at the banners displayed in this temple and sees that of Franklin Lodge alongside the older one of Harmony one cannot but recall another story, both 'sweet and sour' which involved Bro Clegg. It begins with the day of the laying of the hall's foundation stone on 20 April, 1860. Bro Keller, the Provincial Grand Organist and a PM of Shakespeare Lodge, Spilsby, led the Artillery Band at the head of the procession to the Main Ridge site. The sun shone after a showery morning and the proceedings began with the singing of a hymn composed by Dr Walter Clegg for this occasion. The local press, in their report of the proceedings, commented that the only discordant note to mar the pefect 'harmony' of the day was the 'impossibility of recognising the tune owing to the badness of the band', and the lodge minutes of 12 June, 1860 report that 'Bro Clegg was censured for writing to the papers about Keller'.

This unfortunate criticism caused real dissension amongst the brethren and since there had already been some disagreement over who should be WM in this important year some of the Harmony members decided that it was time to establish a separate lodge to meet at the Peacock. That did somehow seem appropriate for what was the result of a fit of 'pique' or pride. That, at least, is how the Franklin Lodge of Boston came into existence and it pursued its own way, in various other locations, for just under a century. WBro J. H. Quayle MBE recounts how: 'When the Franklin Lodge left the White Hart in 1948 their massive oak chairs and tracing board were stored firstly at Fisher Clark's factory and then at Peter Kitwood's Wine & Spirit Stores and finally at Bridge's Farm where we understand that a certain amount of pigeon deposit helped to preserve them'. The centenary brochure however, turns what had continued to be a sour event into something much more sweet. 'Let it be recorded', says the lodge historian, 'to the credit of the Lodge of Harmony, that immediately they heard of our having to leave the High Street Rooms, they offered us accommodation in the Masonic Hall, Main Ridge'. In February 1948 the WMBro R L Tait, spoke for the last time in their old meeting place:

> Next month we shall meet, by courtesy of the WM and brethren of the Lodge of Harmony, in the Masonic Hall, Main Ridge, and we are grateful to them for making it possible for us to meet in a room that has been dedicated and consecrated to the masonic way of life.

He then concluded:

> Brethren, wherever we meet we will always be the Franklin Lodge, so let us carry that true Franklin spirit, which is our constant source of inspiration, to our new meeting place, with the firm resolve in our hearts and minds to go forth in high and united endeavour to extend that Peace, Love and Harmony which is so characteristic of our Order.

That is what they have clearly succeeded in doing ever since and one can only rejoice that they once more found a common resting place where the building takes its pattern from the Temple of 'Dandour' which means 'The abode of the Divine'.

Looking towards the west. The candles are positioned in front of each pedestal with the tracing board mounted on an easel to the far right of the photograph.

COLCHESTER

A Masonic Hall in the Town of Old King Cole

IF YOU TAKE THE new ring road skirting the centre of Colchester on your way in from Chelmsford you will at one point see a two-aisled mediaeval church on a small rise on your right-hand side. It is one of the 16 parish churches that were once serving the population of this ancient borough. In 1952 the growing need to reduce the number of these churches needing regular upkeep by local congregations led to 5 of the church buildings being passed over into secular hands. Two of them, All Saints in the High Street and Holy Trinity with its Saxon tower, were successfully converted into museums of Natural History and Country Life respectively. Another, St Nicholas, a fine Victorian Gothic building by the well-known architect Sir Giles Gilbert Scott, was demolished in 1955—to make way for a supermarket; whilst a fourth, St Martin's, survives as a hall for plays and meetings. The St John Ambulance Brigade used the remaining church as a store for some 20 years but when they at last no longer needed it there was—literally on their doorstep—a body of masons who were only too glad to have the chance to use this vacant building.

The reason for this happy coincidence was that just as the church became vacant a new plan to produce the ring road that now lies close by had meant that the previous Colchester Masonic Hall would have to be demolished. A new home was required and the brethren who had met there eagerly grasped the chance to acquire this centre despite the many and somewhat tedious hurdles that had to be overcome before they could acquire possession from the ecclesiastical authorities.

St Giles Church stands outside the original walled town and is very close to what was St John's Abbey, whose tenants and servants it is thought to have served. Like most mediaeval churches it is a mixture of architectural styles and one can still perceive in it features from the twelfth to the twentieth centuries. After the Reformation the site of the Abbey passed to the Lucas family who made St Giles their chapel. The family that thus occupied the old Abbey were regarded as one of the wealthiest and most cultured in the kingdom and it was said of them that 'all the men were brave and all the women chaste'.

Since those who now occupy the building count loyalty to their sovereign a prime requirement it is worth recording that during the seige of Colchester, in the Civil War of the seventeenth century, one of the Royalist commanders was Sir Charles Lucas. He, with another Royalist, was later condemned to death, shot and buried privately in this church. A large black slab was placed there with an inscription ending '... for their eminent loyalty to their Sovereign ... were ... in

St Giles Masonic Centre, previously a church.

cold blood barbarously murdered.' When an objection to those words was lodged with the restored Charles II by the son-in-law of General Fairfax the King asked the only surviving Lord Lucas what he should do. The answer came that of course he could allow the words 'Lucas and De Lisle were barbarously murdered for their loyalty to King Charles I and his son ordered the memorial of their loyalty to be erased.' Charles II is reputed to have commanded the letter to be engraved doubly deep.

The present conversion of the church to another use has been skilfully made by Mr F. S. Clater, a local architect, and the structural problems have been solved by making the converted building serve a dual purpose, though leaving the whole exterior unchanged. The ground floor, originally the nave and chancel with a side aisle and chapel, is now a dining area. The upper floor, formerly the gallery, is a masonic temple. Because the upper room area does not extend over the whole downstairs area the diners below have a very real sense of being in a mediaeval dining place when they take their seats at supper. The east window adds to that feeling.

One of the most fascinating features of this converted church is the wooden spiral staircase of intriguing design that connects the two floors. It is housed in what was once the wooden bell tower, and half way up it is an illuminated stained glass window which was a masonic memorial to the coronation of Edward VII who was, as we have been reminded elsewhere, a most active freemason and a Past Master of No. 1901 (see King's Lynn, in this volume). The window here was taken from St James the Great Church, East Hill and once more emphasises the fact, so easily to be forgotten in these days, that there are a great many parish and other churches in England that have abundant links with and references to Freemasonry as part of their past.

Along the walls of the temple are displayed four plaques representing the Virtues, which were taken from the Angel Inn that once stood in the High Street and was the original home for Colchester's oldest lodge, founded in 1735. Behind the Master's chair, fixed to the walls, are three old tracing boards which are unveiled for each degree. Here is a connection with the past that is much to be commended and one that must have pleased the Most Worshipful the Grand Master, HRH the Duke of Kent, when he came to open the centre officially in 1976.

As we have seen in other visits to masonic halls in this series this is not the only church building to be adapted for use by freemasons (see Beverley, Warwick and Langport), but it is almost certainly the only *ancient* parish church to be so converted into a hall though an early 19th century one in Shrewsbury has been so used. As might have been expected there were some in the General Synod of the Church of England who objected to such a use for this previous place of worship though the fact that other church buildings locally were to be used for purely secular purposes, whilst this was to be kept in continual existence by men who profess a belief in the Deity, seems to have escaped their notice. To those who regularly find themselves at labour in this building the only experience is one of profound gratitude that they can meet in such an historic and holy place and continue within its walls a fellowship that owes a great deal of its meaning to the example of those very operative masons who built such shrines in the first place. Indeed, one of the previous church wardens is still a practising freemason here.

What makes this hall as equally memorable as the somewhat unique nature of its original use is the sense of historic continuity in Colchester that the lodges now using it have brought with them. Those who want to pursue the story in detail will do well to read the history of the Province written by the late Keith S. Buck and from that story we can select just a few snapshots of local development.

Freemasonry gained its first foothold in Essex in 1735 and in this very town which was then the country's oldest and largest centre with a population of about 9000 inhabitants and with many of them involved in the local cloth trade. Indeed the first recorded meeting was at the 'Three Cups' on Wednesday, 25 November. The sixth founder of the lodge was actually a weaver. A warrant may have been issued to the lodge but the inventories of 1744 and 1757 do not mention it and the oldest possession of that lodge is a combined Bible and Prayer Book of 1629 presented to the members by Thos. Brand, the weaver. It is still in use today in this hall, and as we have seen elsewhere it bears on some of its internal pages the stains of spilled liquid refreshment which would have occupied the same table on which it was first kept.

The large tracing boards dominate the view behind the master's pedestal while ancient wall plaques above and to the left can be seen.

In 1752 the lodge moved to the Angel Inn and was shortly afterwards visited by Lord Carysfort, the Grand Master, who probably came to dedicate the new 'Lodge Room'. From this move arose the present title of the lodge for in 1757 a new set of bye-laws are shown in the Minutes as being approved by the Master, Wardens and brethren of the Angel Lodge—the name which the lodge has retained to this day.

In 1776 we read of the ubiquitous Thomas Dunckerley appearing at the dedication of the first Freemasons' Hall in London as Provincial Grand Master for Essex and No 64 Angel appears as the first of the four lodges that he took over. That was on 23 May and Dunckerley let no time pass before making his impression on the county. On 11 June 1776 there is a warrant for the Lodge of Union to meet at the King's Head, Headgate, Colchester and by July he had constituted it in person. He was its first Honorary Member and appointed Bro Thomas Boggis, a wealthy and respected cloth merchant and its first Junior Warden, as his Deputy Provincial Grand Master. He also made the Revd William Martin Leake, the first Master, his Provincial Grand Secretary.

As a presage to the rightful use of a church as a local Masonic Hall it is worth noting the mention in the *Chelmsford Chronicle* for 1782 of the Anniversary gathering of the Provincial Grand Lodge of Colchester on 16 June. It reads in part:

> ... a respectable number of brethren were present. Several ladies of this place and neighbourhood honoured the society with their company to a public breakfast after which they were introduced by the Stewards and permitted to see the regalia and form of the lodge, when THOMAS DUNCKERLEY, esq, P.G.M. addressed them on the occasion; after the ladies had withdrawn the Brethren proceeded in open Lodge (sic) with the great lights, Bible, book of constitutions, etc. carried by the proper brethren to St Peter's church, when prayers were read by the Rev John Firebrace, MA, a Provincial Grand Chaplain, and an excellent sermon preached by the Rev W. M. Leake, LL.B ...
> A collection was made in the church of £9 1s 6d for the poor of St Peter's Parish.

It was this same day that the Provincial Grand Master provided Angel Lodge with the precious warrant that they needed and which is displayed to this day.

In 1853 the Angel Lodge was to be the preserver of the account of an Especial Provincial Grand Lodge convened at the Three Cups for the purpose of laying the foundation stone of St Mary Magdalene Church. This was carried out with full masonic honours in the presence of 86 Essex brethren and 54 visitors, and was preceded yet again by a church service. The newly encroaching railway provided cheap tickets for the brethren from elsewhere and a 'bath-chair was made available for the PGM, a sign of his increasing infirmity'. The growth of the Province was now to begin in earnest and in 1856 a petition for the United Lodge No 998 to meet at the George Hotel, Colchester was heard. On 8 June 1857 it was duly consecrated at the Town Hall. That made 10 lodges but by the beginning of the nineteenth century there were 50. The first masonic hall built for the purpose appeared at Kelveden in 1895 and by 1907 there is mention of the Masonic Hall at Colchester and of an organ being installed there as a tribute to Claude Egerton Egerton-Green, Banker, Alderman and late Mayor of Colchester.

The meeting of the Angel Lodge for its Bicentenary in 1935 had to be in the Moot Hall and it was there that United Lodge no 697 met for its centenary in 1957.

These were, of course, specially large gatherings and the normal meetings still took place in the centre which is provided. It was only the still further development of the town and its need to preserve its older parts by providing a by-pass that led eventually to the purchase of the present site, its ancient church building and its limited but well-developed facilities in an area where Church and Craft have for so long been in association.

The stairs window in the tower.

IPSWICH

The Masonic Hall in an Ancient Suffolk Seaport

TEN MASONIC LODGES, four Chapters and numerous higher degrees and other masonic Orders now regularly meet in Freemasons Hall, Soane Street, Ipswich, which was originally built in 1879. But as you move about the building or attend one of the older lodges meeting there, you will find plenty of evidence of Masonic activity stretching right back to 1762.

Looking back after more than 200 years we can see that the newly-commenced reign of George III was to end in the rise of a new kind of country—the fresh young republic of the United States. The Empire, which was being promoted by Wolfe and Clive's exploits, was to be the perfect market-place for that industrialised Britain which had not quite begun but which was to create a brash society of secularised concerns; and war, which had at last been suppressed on the home front, was to engage the men of this land for the next 50 years until Napoleon was himself quashed. Indeed, it was in the very week of the founding of the 'Union' Lodge here that the 72nd Regt left the port of Ipswich for Portugal in a struggle with Spain.

It was on 21 January, 1762 that seven brethren received a Warrant from Lord Aberdour, the Grand Master of the premier Grand Lodge, that he would permit them to meet 'at the sign of the Green Man' (that well known figure of ancient English ancestry) in the Parish of St Mary Key. The name 'British Union Lodge' was not adopted until 1777, but the lodge has worked continuously in Ipswich since its inception.

We know singularly little about the founders of this lodge although one of them, John Concom, did live at the Green Man, and was probably the landlord, so one wonders if he was the cause of them settling there. His tombstone in St Mary Key's churchyard is now illegible but a previous incumbent in 1883 took the trouble to record what was then left visible and in the south west corner he found a stone with the letters 'In memory of Jo. . . Couco . . .' and an armorial shield which appears to depict a chevron between three castles—the arms of the premier Grand Lodge, then so much more freely used by both private masons and lodges.

Of the other founders one at least John Clarke, had a strong Ipswich connection, whilst two of the others are mentioned as having been initiated in Angel Lodge, Colchester in 1759 and 1760. The idea of reviving masonry in Ipswich may have come from memories of a still earlier lodge constituted at the White Horse in Tavern Street, in 1730. It had ceased only in 1754, well within the active memory of the new lodge's petitioners. There may also have been talk at the quayside, which was quite close to the Green Man, about masonry in other ports, as we know that John Prentice, one of the founders, was a shipwright, and that by the middle of 1762 a Captain John Softley, of Sunderland, was to be 'made Mason'.

One little sidelight on the early practices of an 18th century lodge which are often described, but for which actual evidence is rarely given, is shown in the lodge minutes for 6 May 1777: 'To Bro William Paxman for his fee drawg. Lodge 4/-' proving that it was indeed customary for the design to be drawn in chalk on the floor or on a Trestle Board by the Tyler. Another entry on 7 May, 1775, which records the payment of 4/- to each of the two brethren for their services as 'operative masons' also reveals that after the ceremony the candidate and/or another 'junior' would be required to erase the same with a mop and pail.

Yet already by 1777 there was a desire for better premises and Right Worshipful Master (*sic*) moved that they go to Bro John Philby's Coffee House. It was passed by ten votes to three. It was here that the name of British Union Lodge was chosen, instead of always carrying the name of the tavern in which they met. By the end of that century the lodge had moved several times more until, as in 1800, they recognise the problem more acutely. A minute for 1 July reads: 'Ipswich races on this date. No accommodation to be had to hold a lodge. Postponed'. By 1816 the lodge felt that they again needed better accommodation and as the Bear & Crown could provide what they wanted they moved there. Then in 1840 a further move was made to the New Assembly Rooms, staying there for nine years until in 1849 they moved to the White Horse. But in 1852 we read in the minutes of 29 December that 'As the landlord of the White Horse Tavern could not make it convenient to provide a satisfactory and proper place for the furniture of the Lodge, it was resolved to hold the next Lodge meeting at the New Assembly Rooms . . .'. The landlord soon found it convenient to make space, but it was not a long term solution, even though Bro Guiver, the next landlord, allowed them to use a more spacious apartment. In the next ten years there were to be several more moves between the White Horse and the New Assembly Rooms.

The pattern of similar difficulties occurs in the case of St Luke's and Perfect Friendship. St Luke's Lodge received its warrant of confirmation from the Earl of Atholl in 1803 and has also worked continuously in Ipswich ever since. St Luke's was originally a military lodge, as the Warrant of Confirmation states that its warrant was first installed in the Eighth Regiment of Foot in 1797, and was later transferred to the Second Regiment of the Royal Lancashire Militia. It is known that for a time this unit was stationed in the town when a number of local residents became members. The Lodge of Perfect Friendship which still works here, was warranted in 1824, though there was an earlier lodge of a similar name warranted by the premier Grand Lodge in 1785 which worked until 1820, but was then absorbed into St Luke's.

The first settled home of St Luke's was at an inn 'known by the sign of the Duke of York' but it could not have remained there long, for in March 1806 a proposition was made that it be removed from the Curriers Arms to the Bear & Crown. In 1837 the lodge moved again and had two more moves before 1856. The original 'Perfect Friendship Lodge' (*sic*) began at the Green Man but for some 60 years it also moved about. From 1851 and for some years it alternated like the British Union, between the White Horse and the New Assembly Rooms. Thus by

The alcove in the main temple with decorated Master's chair.

the middle of the nineteenth century it was clear that there was a pressing need for a permanent meeting place for Ipswich masons.

During these early years British Union Lodge and Perfect Friendship shared many happy times: joint meetings, addresses of congratulations on special occasions, processions to church, even going to the theatre in full regalia, and so forth. But owing to the intense rivalry between the two Grand Lodges up to their union in 1813, there was no such harmony between, on the one hand, British Union and Perfect Friendship, which were both 'Modern' lodges and, on the other, St Luke's which was an 'Ancient' Atholl Lodge. After the Union in 1813 the position soon changed. For instance, it is recorded that in 1843 the Master of British Union invited the members of St Luke's and Perfect Friendship to assist him at the laying of the foundation stone of the new Custom House of the Port of Ipswich. This building, which still exists, was erected on the quay of the new Wet Dock which had been constructed six years earlier and was then the largest wet dock in the country. It is a most impressive building, the front elevation being of classical design with a four column portico of the Tuscan order.

Unfortunately, this period of fraternal relationship was not to last. In 1863 a serious schism occured among the members of the Lodge of Perfect Friendship (belying its name!) and a number of its brethren petitioned for a new Lodge in Ipswich. Although this was not backed by either British Union or St Luke's, a new Lodge called the 'Prince of Wales' Lodge was consecrated the same year. Scarcely more than a year later the members of this lodge were feeling that it would be a fine and proper thing to have their own premises. Enquiries were made of lodges all over the country to help in deciding what was required, and a plot of land was bought in St Stephen's Church passage running between St Stephen's Lane and Brook Street. Plans were prepared and a scheme was proposed to raise £1200 in proportions of £300 from each of the four lodges in the town, *viz* British Union, St Luke's, Perfect Friendship and Prince of Wales. Although, as we have seen earlier, it was clear that there was a pressing need for a meeting place for Masonry, the three older lodges—no doubt because of the circumstances in which the Prince of Wales came into existence—declined to cooperate. Nevertheless Prince of Wales Lodge pressed ahead and in less than a month raised £1,070 on its own. The hall, an elegant building very similar in size and layout to the original part of the present hall, was soon built, much of the work and most of the furniture being contributed by brethren of the lodge. It was consecrated in January 1866. However, it was not until later that the three older lodges transferred to it as follows:

British Union	1867
Perfect Friendship	1870
St Luke's	1877

Regrettably the hall soon ran into financial difficulties and at the end of 1877 was sold. It has never since been used for Masonic purposes but, after being damaged in the last war, is still in other use today.

However, it was not long before another committee of all four lodges was formed, under the chairmanship of Bro William Boby, to procure some new premises. Bro William Boby had been initiated in British Union Lodge in 1855. It

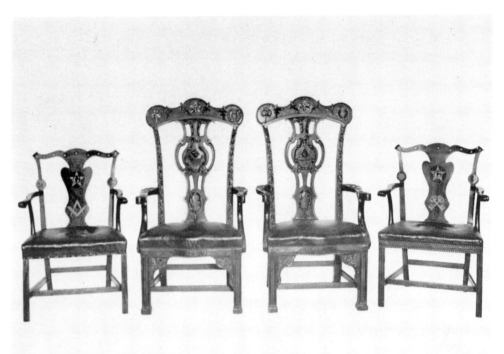

The 'Beade', 'Baines' and 'Sadd' chairs.

was he who was the founder of the special 'Feast of Roses' first recorded in 1863 when the banquet room was to be profusely decorated with roses of all shades and sizes. The tables, walls and parts of the ceiling were to represent a bower of the bloom, and the celebration was to replace the earlier and traditional midsummer St John's Festival. He was also the owner of a snuff box which is still passed round the lodge after supper. The work done by this committee was very effective for by 3 April, 1879, the first meeting of a lodge was taking place in a new hall in Soane Street, Ipswich.

This building, still in use, has a straightforward brick facing with a large and impressive sandstone, pillared doorway in the lower centre, with its own heavy triangulated pediment and double blue doors. It is flanked by two tall sash windows in white. In the angles to the left and right of the arched door casing are pentagrams carved in stone and in the triangular pediment space is a Knight Templar Lorraine Cross.

Above the three identical sash windows of the first floor is another triangular gable end with a stone circular feature at its centre, and this contains the Royal Arch sign of three juxtaposed 'Taus'. This building by itself, would present a fine appearance but alongside this front and to the right is another façade of quite different appearance which was an early twentieth century addition. Here we have a wide, open arch of brick headed by a large keystone and with three steps leading up and inwards to what is now the main entrance, the white walls of which set a sharp contrast to the exterior. Above the keystone there is a slender base extending the whole width of this extension and this supports two large stone pillars reaching up almost to the full height of this frontage. The whole of the area between them is of plain and stained glass showing masonic emblems to passers by. Its white mullions of timber are set off by the lower delicate portico-style frame that resembles a doorway of glass. Between 1974 and 1977 the whole of these premises were restored, and extended, by embodying and altering an early nineteenth century dwelling house adjoining the twentieth-century addition referred to above.

Now let us move up the steps and through the entrance doors into the spacious foyer of the hall, and experience the warm reception it conveys. Notice, facing you, the Edwardian oak panelling and overmantel with Ionic columns supporting a pediment. To the right stands an interesting nineteenth-century long case clock locally made, as the name on the face 'George Weller—Yoxford' states. Now turn about to examine the engraved glass door panels—filled with decorations. One panel contains Hebrew characters and an elevated banner, whilst the other shows

The Tyler's Jewel: obverse (left) *and reverse* (right).

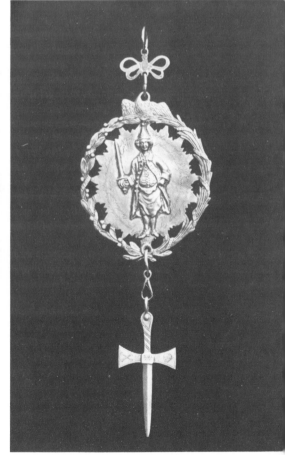

three columns of the Ionic, Doric and Corinthian Orders respectively. Both sets of designs are enclosed in a wavy cable of rope. Contemplate the impressive massive oak staircase with wide moulded handrail and turned bulbous balusters.

After you have left your coat and hat in the accommodation to the right, glance into the small committee room through a doorway leading off the hall. This is a small intimate room with some simple plasterwork and other decorations of early nineteenth century. It is furnished with an oak gate-legged table probably of the same period, and some suitable chairs.

Return now to the entrance hallway, ascend the first flight of the wide and gently rising staircase and turn off to the left and up a few stairs to a doorway lettered in gold 'The Watson Room'. On entering this spacious and inviting chamber, which is mainly used for Lodges of Instruction, you will see standing against the opposite wall, a fine Chippendale style bookcase flanked on either side with display cases containing a large and interesting well-captioned collection of Masonic Jewels, including early Master Masons' jewels up to 1840 and two rare Royal Arch jewels of 1804 and 1829. The collection was, in the main, presented by WBro R. B. Skippen of Corinthian Lodge. The bookcase has a plate on it which reads 'Presented to British Union Lodge in memory of WBro S. F. Watson PGStB, 1977'. The cost of the bookcase, together with the cost of completely furnishing the room, was generously met by his widow. The bookcase now contains the library of Masonic books which had belonged to WBro Watson, as well as others belonging to the lodge.

Among the many volumes in this library will be found a first edition of Anderson's *Constitutions* published in 1723 (a volume elegantly bound in black calf, gilt tooled and fitted with two clasps), *A Short View of the History of Freemasonry* by William Sandys published in 1829 and a Second Edition of Preston's *Illustrations*. Another item is a booklet that contains the address by the Revd F. W. Freeman, MA at the consecration of the Phoenix Lodge, Stowmarket, on the subject of 'Let us not be weary in well doing'. He certainly believed in what he preached for it was a discourse so splended that it reached 16 pages and was later printed and sold on behalf of the Royal Masonic Benevolent Annuity Fund. Other lodges, of course, also have books of their own and housed in the basement of the hall are many well-indexed records and documents in the care of a brother who acts as an archivist for the Province of Suffolk.

Returning now to the main staircase, proceed on upwards past the large front array of windows rising above. It is from within that one specially notices the squares, compasses, trowels and plumblines that make up the window decoration. On gaining the landing, which also acts as an ante-room for the temple, notice the oak gate-legged table of considerable antiquity used for 'Presence' (or Attendance) Books. Also there is a large comfortable upholstered settee which is much appreciated by some elderly brethren waiting to enter the lodge. Leading off the landing is 'a convenient room adjoining the lodge' which, in addition to being used for the preparation of candidates, serves as a room in which brethren clothe themselves with their masonic regalia. At the far end of this room note the handsome Sheraton sideboard on which stands a pair of large, heavily ornamented and gilded vases of Meissen style with circular insets of charmingly painted floral scenes. Notice also the small pillars and emblems on or above the overmantel of the fireplace. An item of special interest above the fireplace is a cut-out moulded

solid brass plate depicting the square and compasses in the M.M. position. A
caption against this records that in bygone days it was customary to affix such
plates to the coffins of masons. Among the numerous tastefully framed masonic
warrants and certificates which adorn the walls there is also an engraving which is
a full length portrait of the Earl of Atholl, who was Grand Master of the
'Antients'. This was presented to St Luke's Lodge at a joint meeting of the five
East Anglian 'Atholl' lodges at Norwich on 16 May, 1953.

At last it is time to enter the temple. In a position to the left of the door as you
enter is a marble plaque which reads 'This Temple was renovated in 1974 with a
bequest of £5000 from WBro Charles Dalton PAGDC and other donations and
voluntary work'. The décor of the temple cannot fail to make an immediate impact
on every brother. The crimson and blue pattern surrounding the prominent
pavement of specially woven carpet; the rows of benches and seats upholstered in
blue cloth and backed by white painted wall panelling, personally hand-made and
fixed by WBro George Scott of British Union Lodge; the soft lighting from
chandeliers and wall brackets; all combine with the masonic furnishings and
properties described below, to provide a perfect setting for masonic proceedings.

Spaced along the North and South walls above the panelling are shields hand
painted with the emblems of the ten lodges using the hall, all of whom supported
the 1974 − 7 restoration as follows:

114	British Union	1762
225	St Luke's	1803
376	Perfect Friendship	1824
969	Prince of Wales	1863
3093	Corinthian	1905
4254	Gippeswyk	1921
5922	Ionic	1943
6347	Perfect Amity	1946
6637	Orwell	1948
6829	Christchurch	1949

The total financial cost of restoration and extension amounted (in 1977) to
nearly £70,000, most of which was raised in four years by these lodges.

Now notice the magnificent Master's chair. This belongs to the Lodge of Perfect
Friendship and is undoubtedly the most outstanding piece of furniture in the hall
and is thought to date from the mid-eighteenth century. Clearly designed to
complement this chair are two others which stand on the left and right of it. They
were purchased by British Union lodge in 1934 with the proceeds of a legacy of
WBro J. W. Owen Baines MBE. All three chairs have slender-framed and richly
carved backs with bulbous headrests. The Master's chair has a glory in gold at the
centre of this headrest, flanked by a smooth ashlar with cramp and keystone on its
side. In the two rounded ends are, on the left a sun with a face, and on the right a
crescent moon with a face looking inwards. Below the glory is a delicate and
interwoven set of masonic tools with a coat of arms of the premier Grand Lodge
beneath, and yet further down a fine beehive surrounded by bees. The Baines
chairs are very similar save that their headrests have a rose at the centre, a
shamrock on the left and a thistle on the right, these being floral emblems of

The main temple looking west. The distinctive pillars and globes are gilded with an unusual cradle to support the globes.

British Union Lodge. In the centre of the back rest of one chair is an all-seeing eye; on the other a pair of compasses on a segment of a circle with a glory between.

These three chairs stand within a classical style alcove of two pilasters bearing a semicircular arch with a keystone showing a crown at its height. The keystone is flanked with another stone showing an all-seeing eye on the left and a book opened on a glory on the right. The ceiling of the alcove is painted blue with stars scattered about but with the Seal of Solomon at the back and just above the rim of the alcove base is a small light that is switched on for the Bright Morning Star.

We have not yet finished with the lovely chairs in this room for to the left of the alcove is a large gilded chair presented by WBro Alloway to Prince of Wales Lodge at the time of its founding in 1863. (It is repositioned as the Master's Chair for meetings of the Prince of Wales Lodge).

Hall exterior in Soane Street.

Above its rather plain and solid oak base, back and arms it has a huge gilded headrest and pediment. The latter is triangular with its lower edge divided by three huge gilded Prince of Wales feathers emerging from a crown. Within the decorated frame below these are two combinations of carved white emblems—the square and compasses in the FC position on the left and a level and plumbline on the right. A small silver plaque describes the origin of the chairs. This Prince of Wales Lodge, of course, was named after HRH Albert Edward, Prince of Wales, Past Grand Master of England. In 1870 he graciously consented to be elected an honorary member of the lodge. (For his further East Anglian Masonic connections see the chapter on King's Lynn).

The Secretary's and Treasurer's chairs, which are in the Chippendale style, are no less elegant. They belong to British Union Lodge and are called the 'Reade' and 'Sadd' chairs after their original donors. The former was given in 1837 and has a lovely inlaid back frame showing the sun and crescent moon, with pentagram, letter G and square and compasses whilst the latter given in 1937 was a replica of the earlier chair save that in place of the square and compasses we have the crossed keys of the Treasurer.

After the closure of the first Masonic Hall in 1877 some of the furniture was sold, but the Prince of Wales Lodge decided that the rest should be retained for use in the new temple. This included the Alloway Master's chair, the two Wardens' chairs and the Scargiola Tables for the Secretary and Treasurer.

The three pedestals which stand before the chairs of the principal officers were made by a Bro Pettit. A metal plaque in Gothic letters on the Master's pedestal reads: 'These three pedestals were made from wood which was part of the old Grammar School Room, Foundation Street, Ipswich, and which room had formerly been the refectory to the Convent of Black Dominicans called Friars Preachers established in the latter part of Henry VIII's reign, 1270'.

Other items which cannot go unnoticed by any visitor to the temple are the 'handsome pair of capitals' which still adorn it. They are wooden, gilded pillars with elaborately decorated capitals showing network over pomegranates, but especially notable for their two globes that are supported above the chapiters by four legged wooden frames. About seven feet high and just at the inner entrance to the temple they at once impress any visitor and serve to remind him of the work in which he is to be involved.

Let us suppose now that it is a meeting of British Union Lodge which the visitor is attending here. On the South wall, above the Secretary's table, the original warrant of the lodge, dated 21 January, 1762, will be proudly displayed. Behind and above the Master's chair will also be displayed the bold and unmistakably patriotic lodge banner (the third in successsion of similar design), a straight-forward Union Jack with a square and compasses in the upper part of the central red cross of St George, the lodge number 114 on the lower part, and across the horizontal arms the bold words 'BRITISH UNION LODGE'. When the name was adopted on 29 July, 1777 the 'British Union' of England and Scotland (Ireland did not join the Union till 1801) was at war with the American colonists, who had made their Declaration of Independence on 4 July, 1776 and thereafter referred to themselves as the 'American Union'. It therefore seems probable that the members of the lodge decided to call it 'British Union Lodge' as a measure of support for their King and Government. When the name 'British Union' was adopted the

Union Flag did not of course contain the red saltire cross of St Patrick, but as the first banner was not acquired until well into the nineteenth century, the Union Jack as we know it today was the design selected.

It was in 1837 that the Lodge's tracing boards were presented by Bro John Reade, another respected member of the lodge, who was to become the Provincial Grand Master of Suffolk later. They are very similar to those evolved by John Harris and adopted by the Emulation Lodge but their special interest here is that they are signed by a local artist, Sam Read, a native of Needham Market. He was later employed by the *Illustrated London News* and was the artist who drew the harrowing scenes of the Crimean War. About the same time a set of silver-mounted ebony gavels—still in use—was presented by Robert Martin.

The VSL used at every meeting of the lodge is a fine specimen of a Geneva Bible, printed by Robert Barker in 1608, beautifully bound in black roan leather and tooled with masonic emblems and lettering in gold. This was presented in 1837 by Robert Deck, a printer and book-seller, who was a member of the lodge for 49 years, and five times its Master. It was he who also presented the first edition of Anderson's *Constitutions* to the lodge library.

Among the unusual jewels proudly worn in the lodge may be mentioned those worn by the IPM, the Inner Guard and the Tyler. From the silver marks on these they were probably presented or acquired in the first years of the nineteenth century. The IPM's jewel has an ornate pair of compasses spanning a segment of a circle, with a fine 'sunface and rays at the centre, and an upturned square above it'. As Inner Guard it was originally the newest EA who kept the door on the inside. In British Union he wore the lodge badge of a trowel which would have seemed to him a familiar masonic emblem. This is still worn by the Inner Guard of the lodge today. Another exceptional jewel belonging to the lodge is that of the Tyler, which was presented on 2 October, 1804 by the then S.W. Bro Thomas Rolfe. On its obverse, and starting from the clasp that links it with a collar, one notes, first a double knot, and then a circular wreath of corn and olives with a pelican feeding its young, by exposing its breast to their beaks at the apex. The wreath encloses a large splayed 'Glory' that covers almost all the intervening space on which are shown a level in the centre, and a square and compasses in the FC position in the upper part. Below, a plumbline separates a miniature tracing board, with a circle, triangle and a four-sided square upon it, and a VSL showing the tooled spine with the remarkable symbol of IHS with a cross, whose upright runs straight through the cross piece of the H on the cover. (This form of IHS symbol is found, incidentally, in many graveyards of the eighteenth century as part of masons' tombstones). From a ring at the bottom of the wreath hangs a poignard. On the reverse, and again below the knot with the back of the pelican visible, the smooth back of the 'Glory' is surrounded with an inscription recording the gift by Rolfe, but at the centre is a most revealing figure. It is a Tyler with a large hilted sword upright in his hand, a tall pointed hat on his head, a long surcoat with 7 buttons, a rich waistcoat and wide, natural lambskin apron that reaches to his knees. His left arm is akimbo, and his feet are as in a regular step. It is a most striking figure which encapsulates a piece of real masonic history. (For other Tylers' hats see Bolton and Berwick in volume three of this series).

It is now time to leave the temple, remove regalia and proceed downstairs 'from labour to refreshment'. In the space for refreshment (which was the original entrance hall), notice the large mirror covering the old doorway. You cannot walk about this hall without being aware of mirrors and their frames—in ivory, gilded wood, or just plain timber—some of them with delightful masonic motifs. Also in this area is a large marble shield surrounded by a heavy rounded oak frame. The engraving on the shield reads 'This Masonic Hall was erected by members of the Lodge Prince of Wales No 959 Ipswich. Foundation stone laid May 1st, 1865. Building finished and consecrated 2 January, 1866'. A small strip below records that this large memorial tablet was removed from the first hall and fixed in the second hall when it was built in 1879. Lower still, a small plaque beneath the 1866 tablet and referring to the second hall reads, 'Ipswich Freemasons erected this Hall in 1879 and restored and extended it between 1974 and 1977'.

After a suitable interval for refreshment before supper, wide double doors will be thrown open and you will move into the dining hall. This again was panelled throughout by WBro George Scott in the 1974-1977 restoration, giving a warm and rich look to the room. It is in recognition of his part in the restoration of the hall that the room has been named 'The George Scott Room', signified by bold gold lettering above the main doors. At the east end of the room behind the top table, notice the circular plaque with a pair of compasses covered by an overflowing cornucopia (a good sign for a dining room) and beneath it a richly coloured representation of the arms of the Borough of Ipswich with two sea horses as supporters. Interesting too are the three delightful chairs for the principal officers at the after proceedings. They came from the Connaught MMM Lodge and were presented by WBro H. A. Westbrook PGD in May 1968.

Each lodge, of course, follows its own customs at the dinner table, which it would be beyond the scope of this paper to detail, but any description of the hall cannot omit to mention the two splended antique glass Loving Cups which were presented to British Union Lodge at its Centenary banquet by Bro Deck. These are heavily engraved with signs and symbols which would repay a close study by any mason. They are passed around the lodge according to ancient ceremony at every Installation.

As a visitor prepares to depart from the hall, he will have experienced a grand masonic occasion in a place of much affection and history, where the principles of Brotherly Love, Relief, and Truth are regularly taught and assuredly practised within a context of being happy and communicating happiness.

The Masonic Hall in the Duke's Head Hotel

KING'S LYNN IS both an ancient and a fascinating place where, says one encyclopaedia, 'The streets are generally narrow and winding, and many of the houses and buildings are renowned for their architectural and historic interest'. It is therefore not surprising to learn that in terms of what might be called the 'Grand Lodge era' of English speculative freemasonry, that is, after 1717, there was a lodge of the ancient Craft established here without much delay. In 1729 the Duke's

Head lodge, No 70, was constituted on 28 September, to meet on the first Friday of each month at the inn of that name in the Market Place. Considering that Lynn was a premier market town and seaport at the mouth of the Great Ouse it is also fitting that the first Master was a Capt Turner, son of Sir Charles Turner, a local merchant, and was himself a Captain of the Trained Bands, as well as a Collector of Customs for the port. Sadly like six other lodges duly founded in the area in the eighteenth century (Star, Sun in the Strand, Friendship, Strict Benevolence, Attention and Union) they were all to cease work by the early nineteenth century and only the Philanthropic Lodge, constituted on 22 March, 1810, survives to this day as the premier lodge of the town.

It is this lodge whose present meeting place is so worth noting today and which is lodged in what is called 'The Masonic Hall, Tuesday Market Place', though it is reached by, and attached to, that same Duke's Head Hotel which was the gathering place 260 years ago. There is thus a very long tradition of assemblage in the building we are to examine and it is with a justifiable sense of pride that the present members of the Philanthropic both use and display their temple.

Before we actually enter it we may usefully look at something of the past history of the lodge and see how, in fact, it came to be finally established here in 1872.

According to the lodge historian, WBro Glasier, a list in the first minute book for 10 January, 1833 gives the membership as 24, ('of whom ten were Master Mariners, one a Baker, one a Coach Smith, one an Innkeeper, one a Shoe maker, one a Stone Mason and nine have no occupations stated'). This predominance of sea-faring men is confirmed by the letter from the Atholl Lodge of Perseverance in Norwich which told the Grand Secretary of the Antients Grand Lodge that they 'had attended at Lynn on Monday, the 14th [May, 1810] and installed the Officers; they had met the Sea Captains and other brethren to the number of twenty, and that the lodge was held at the Maid's Head'. This is to some extent a puzzle for the warrant which they also acknowledged receipt of stated clearly that this new body was 'to be held at the Sun Inn, King's Lynn' and naming the Master and Wardens as usual.

The main temple with numerous certificates and banners displayed on the walls.

This warrant, numbered 142, is a special treasure of the lodge for it is one of only two in the whole of the Province and is still a rarity in freemasonry generally. The warrant, due to the effects of the Seditious Societies Act, was transferred from a lodge that met at the 'King of Prussia's Head' at Welchpool in Monmouthshire but which had not made returns since 1775, after only one year of foundation! It repays a careful examination for it states that it comes from the Grand Lodge 'according to the old Constitutions granted to his Royal Highness Prince Edwin at York, Anno Domino Nine hundred twenty and five' in the name of 'Prince John, Duke, Marquis and Earl of Atholl', and appointing those officers named until the next Installation, that 'to be upon (or near) every ST JOHN'S DAY during the continuance of the lodge for ever'. Its meeting days were to be the first and third Mondays in every month.

Two especial matters of interest connected with this document are that it meant that the new lodge had an earlier number than its mother lodge, though warranted 15 years after it! Whilst Bro Gage, the first Worshipful Master, was to leave King's Lynn the very next year and assist in forming the Grand Lodge of Wigan of which he was the Deputy Grand Master from 1823 to 1842. (This breakaway body was established because of the objection raised by some lodges in that area of Lancashire to the pretensions and alterations consequent upon the Union of the Antients and Moderns Grand Lodges and the powers granted to the then United Grand Lodge.) It can already be understood why an examination of the contents of the present 'hall' is both instructive and memorable. The number of the lodge was itself changed at the Union to 172.

A letter in the lodge file at Great Queen Street, London, makes clear that questions were asked about why the lodge was not meeting where stated in the warrant. The answer of Bro Gage, and we now know his ilk, was that it had not seemed expedient, but no other reason was given and it appears that Grand Lodge was not determined to pursue the matter. For 18 years the lodge remained at the Maid's Head but from then until 1859 they moved from the Star to the East Anglian and thence to the Globe. On 10 October, 1859 'the Lodge removed to the Duke's Head, because the Landlord thereof was a brother, while he of the Globe was not'.

It was to be a period of occupation with its own distinctive features for on 4 March, 1861 'it was resolved to have a bespeak at the Theatre, the Worshipful Master and the Brethren to appear in Masonic Costume (sic); a similar resolution was carried in 1862, and in 1866; this is the latest instance which I have found in which the Brethren of any Lodge in this Province appeared at a Theatre in Masonic Clothing.' (Glasier p.30) In 1864 we also have the sad exclusion of a brother for eloping with the wife of a brother member. By December they were back at the Globe. It was then that the lodge voted ten pounds towards establishing a lodge library, which was for the next 50 years a most exceptional thing for any Norfolk lodge to do.

It is now, in May 1870, that the lodge had the special pleasure of electing as a joining member no less a person than HRH the Prince of Wales, the future Edward VII. From that time until the end of his reign he continued to be a subscribing member and it is therefore a matter of real delight that on the walls of the present temple are documents showing this exceptional connection. To receive his Royal Highness the lodge held an emergency meeting on 4 February, 1871 at which his attendant Private Secretary, Bro Francis Knollys, CB was passed to the second degree, having been initiated the previous year in the Westminster and Keystone Lodge No 10. A year later, in 1872, the lodge chose two of its members, the Rev. William Lake Onslow and Francis Knollys, to convey to HRH their congratulations on his having recovered from a severe illness. They apparently met him in a 'small inner room with doors closed', gave him the signs in the three degrees and then read the address.

It is with this connection very much in mind that we come to the present lodging, again the Duke's Head Hotel, to which the lodge returned on 4 November, 1872. Here, in this intimate and well-appointed lodge room, a future King of England conducted ceremonies and sat at ease with his fellow masons—an experience not shared by many and certainly by very few on a regular basis. As one looks around, considering its location, the appeal of the place can well be understood. For this Masonic Hall is distinguished by being, in effect, simply one large room. Its security and privacy is guaranteed.

A view of the main temple showing the wardens' chairs and the entrance porchway.

The room is situated at the rear of the Duke's Head but is approached through a special door from the upper corridors of the hotel proper and all that separates the visitor from the temple is a mere passage or ante-chamber to be used for signing the register and preparing the candidate. The entrance door to the temple proper is at the extreme western end of the temple's north wall and at the angle with the west wall. The temple when entered, therefore, stretches out to one's right. The most unusual factor on entering, however, is that you pause on a small dais of three steps above the floor of the lodge, and under a most impressive porchway supported by four carved pillars. It is very much as if one were making a dramatic entry and the candidate, blindfolded, must make a very telling sight as he is challenged and tested in full view of the brethren seated below. In terms of entering a 'Temple' by a 'porchway or entrance' it is certainly the most effective feature in England that I know.

The inside porch of the temple.

It would have served to great effect when, as on 26 January 1885, HRH attended Norfolk's Provincial Grand Lodge, and had 10 special stewards to escort him. To see his portly but distinguished figure appear in the Masonic Hall doorway would have been no less impressive. The room he would look down upon would have pleased him no less.

The chairs of the Worshipful Master and Wardens are of oak, are very elegant and very old. They are either Chippendale or Sheraton and have their appropriate emblems, the square and compasses, level and plumbline. There is no information as to how they came into the possession of the lodge and it is generally believed that they were bequeathed by, or bought from, one of the many Lynn lodges that lapsed. If so, then this is a precious link with a still older local masonry.

The collar jewels of the principal officers are of silver, that of the WM bearing a hallmark of 1807, and others that of 1809, suggesting perhaps that they were the ones sent with the warrant especially for the lodge's inauguration. There is also a silver jewel in the form of a trowel which used to be worn by the Inner Guard, hallmarked 1809. This indicates a very old practice, repeated in a Norwich lodge, in that it was the implement presented to the new candidate at the north-east corner when he is spoken to there, thence invested with the trowel, and made to act as Inner Guard, as we know that a new member was so instructed in eighteenth century Antients' working. When the practice stopped the jewel remained with the now annually appointed Inner Guard, to seal up the inner porch and preserve silence and harmony within.

We also discover here that the Immediate Past Master's jewel is different to that normally worn elsewhere. It shows a pair of compasses resting on the segment of a circle, with a flaming sun between the compass legs. The deacons also have mercury figures with wings, caps and the caduceus, or serpent-entwined staff with wings attached.

The lodge room, tastefully decorated in a style that befits its nineteenth century origin, is throughout enriched by the many items that adorn the walls—the wavy sword on the rear wall, or the silk banner first given in 1859, the two small certificates of 1806 and 1819, and a more evidently Antients certificate with the words, 'Holiness to the Lord', of 1812. The two globes, a part of so many of the older lodge rooms which we have visited, are set against the wall at the east end and there is, also framed, an old apron made especially for use in this very lodge and showing the number, 107. There is one of those Bell's masonic charts which can so engross the masonic student with all the symbols of many degrees, and there is also a cast iron gravestone cover made by Aickman which suggests a rather more realistic practice of one of the degrees. Two sets of tracing boards were presented by Bro Cummings in 1857 and by Bro Wilkin two decades later, but the really striking first degree tracing board was handed to the lodge by Bro Broadfoot, in 1847. This very eminent brother, a Past Master of the Lodge of Stability, No 217, in London, and a founder of the oldest lodge of instruction in Stability working, had served in the Lodge of Reconciliation in 1813. His gift to the lodge was therefore a most precious heirloom and it is good to see that it is treated with great respect even to this day.

Whilst it is true that this Masonic Hall must be amongst the most restricted in size and does not have any great claim to architectural spectacle yet its associations with persons and periods of the past, together with the fact that it must be one of the very few lodge rooms connected with a hotel which is allowed to leave its possessions out in permanent arrangement, make it a most noteworthy part of our Craft family and a lodge centre to remember.

One last possession of the lodge that dwells here may perhaps close this all too brief visit by drawing together the threads of the years we have transversed. It is a lodge summons for Friday 9 February, 1821, signed by Sir M. B. Folkes, 'Right Worshipful Master', requiring a Bro Lawson to attend at the Coffee House, Lynn, the place of meeting for the Lodge of Friendship, then No 158.

This Master was a relative of Sir William Hovel Browne ffolkes, Bart. who was first the WM of Philanthropic lodge in 1880, and both of them were the descendants of that Sir William ffolkes whose blood brother was Martin ffolkes of Hillington, President of the Royal Society and Deputy Grand Master of England under the Duke of Richmond in 1724-5. Not only so but WBro ffolkes' family was connected by marriage with Sir John Turner, for Sir Martin Browne ffolkes married the latter's daughter in January 1775. It was with the Turner family that we made our first acquaintance with Freemasonry in Lynn in 1729, and the Masonic Hall which we have just visited forms part of the Duke's Head Hotel which was originally the residence of the Turner family. Is it any wonder that as you stand in the lodge room at the rear of that ancient house you are somehow aware of a whole network of masonic links and impressions. It is indeed something to remember.

KNUTSFORD

The Cheshire Masonic Hall in a Barn

IT HAS TAKEN a good deal of effort to protect the country town of Knutsford from the effects of modern traffic. Only the building of the M6 and the diversion of cars and lorries through the western part of the centre has allowed a certain old-world tranquility to return to its old main street which figured so graphically in the book 'Cranford' by Mrs Gaskell. It is something of this same search for a quiet and untroubled spot for a practice of masonry that has led to the creation of a truly memorable Masonic Hall, and perhaps the most modern one in this volume, on the edge of that same town.

Mrs Gaskell was not the only literary figure to be associated with this district. In their day, and they were almost exactly contemporary, she was probably outshone by a member of the aristocracy whose name is still kept alive by his descendants to this day—he was John Byrne Leicester Warren, Baron de Tabley. Educated at Eton and Christchurch, Oxford, he moved in rather different circles to the daughter of a Unitarian minister. By the time that 'Cranford' was appearing he

The original roof blends in well with the modern interior style.

was gaining public acclaim for seven volumes of verse which were considered remarkable for their grace and refinement of feeling. His work 'Philoctetes' was even praised and commented upon by Gladstone and the poet Browning. It revealed his immense knowledge of classical culture, and though later drama and poetry from his pen did not achieve quite the same notoriety he was no less well known as a scholar of botany and of the study of ancient coins, whilst his work on the flora of Cheshire was a final word on the subject.

This polymath was no less an ardent freemason. In 1862 he was the prime mover in the creation of the De Tabley Lodge No 941, and in this he was joined by two other well known Cheshire noblemen—Cornwall Legh and Wilbraham Egerton. Lord de Tabley became in fact the first WM and gave permission for the adoption of the de Tabley coat of arms by the lodge. Two years later, when the Baron was only 30, he was appointed Provincial Grand Master of Cheshire.

The high backed Master's chair contrasts with the wall panelling.

Since that time the tenure of this high office in the county has been in the successive hands of some member or other of the three families just mentioned, until in 1949 the then Provincial GM, Cuthbert Leicester Warren, retired due to ill-health. He had been initiated and raised in the De Tabley Lodge in 1909 and appointed PGM in 1925. It is his son who became the eventual benefactor whose gift made it at last possible for the De Tabley Lodge to have a permanent home of its own.

In the foreword to a booket describing the present premises Lt Col JBL Leicester-Warren has put into words his deep feelings about this development:

'In my forty-three years as a freemason I have been continuously associated with many of the Masonic bodies who meet in Knutsford and many of my happiest memories are connected with them. During all this time and indeed ever since my Great Grandfather started the family interest in Freemasonry in Knutsford, these bodies have never had a permanent home of their own and it has given me the greatest pleasure to find myself in a position to remedy this want'

The want was real. For many years the Assembly Room of the Royal George Hotel in the older part of the town was used for lodge meetings. Older members still recall the discomfort of sitting by the tall, wide windows and receiving the full benefit of the cold air stream which descended from them. The room had always to be cleared away and successive managements were not always as amenable to the requirements as each other. The result was that when the old Council Chambers became available in 1931 the brethren were only too glad to rent them as a meeting place, though the Assembly Room at the hotel still served as a most suitable centre for installation meetings.

The demand for increased rent was but one of the reasons for an ever-growing call by some of the more far-seeing brethren for a 'home' of their own and at last, after examining a number of possibilities, the previous electricity showrooms at Paradise Green were rented and adapted for more stable use. That was in 1963. The longed-for permanent site was not achieved but at least local masons could now catch their breath as they waited for what was to be the crucial next move. It may not have struck them as an omen that they did in fact go to the Angel for dinner.

Eventually, in 1967, Col Leicester-Warren began to have the notion that some redundant land and farm buildings at White House Farm, Bexton, near to the southern boundary of Knutsford Urban District, might possibly be the answer. The building had been used as a shippon, the ground floor full of cement cattle stalls, together with the iron work so essential for controlling the beasts that were to be housed there. A plank floor above this area had been used for storing cattle food and hay, etc. and there was an old unsafe staircase leading to this upper storey. It looked and seemed an impossible task to envisage even this offer as a future home that would be worthy of the De Tabley name. Yet it *was* theirs—and in two years of remarkable hard work it was a Masonic Hall with a future.

The Deed of Gift embraced some 5000 square yards of land, formerly attached to the farm, the shippon and storage already mentioned, two loose boxes, a Dutch barn and an implement shed. An initial brief survey at least established that in the shippon area there was sufficient accommodation for masonic ceremony, the storage of special furniture for Mark and Chapter, Knight Templar and Rose Croix, and the requirements for heating. The only problem was the narrowness of the existing structure, only 20′ from wall to wall. It was at once decided to create another third as much floor area that could be separated from the rest by a folding partition, thus giving flexibility of use according to the particular masonic unit that might wish to occupy the hall on each occasion.

It was at this point that a brick pillar had to be introduced to reduce the span of the necessary new steel framing and form an attachment for the partition folds. What was quite apparent was that the existing roof and trusses—the craft of carpenters doing a fine job a century before—had such character and interest that it should be left open to view and maintain the simple nature of the original shed.

Opposite: *The De Tabley pre-Union banner*

The demolished loft floor provided just the wood needed for the new roof extension and the demolished side wall enabled the bricks to be used in their new setting.

Only those who have planned such an alteration and worked to incorporate damp proofing, insulation, artificial lighting and decoration can possibly guess what was involved. The work was organised on the basis of professional *and* voluntary labour all provided by masonic brethren, and following the commencement of work on 23 June, 1968 a vast number of jobs were tackled and overcome. Woodworm beetle was attacked, demolition carried out, draining was devised, flooring was laid, panelling was prepared and fitted and not a little outside gardening had also to be done.

The seating was met by the generous provision of 100 cinema seats, but they had to be given new covers and their metal frames repainted. The lavatories had to be tiled and the new drive and usefully large car park had to be levelled and tarmacked. The 'professionals' concreted the floor, plastered the walls, installed the oil-fired ducted air heating and put the necessary finishing touches to the car park. Thus, at last, the first stage of turning this fine gift of somewhat unprepossessing buildings into a Masonic Hall had been accomplished and an old lodge had a meeting place in keeping with its history, name and traditions. It must have been a very contented, if also somewhat exhausted group of brethren who sat down just once more at the Angel on 8 September, 1969 for the Dedication banquet.

They surely deserved the shellfish, asparagus soup, salmon, sorbet, coq au vin, sweet, cheese and coffee. I am not surprised that on one such menu the happy diner has written against the *Cassata Denise*-2 portions!! By the time they had washed it all down with sherry, white and red wine, port or brandy, they could go home content. Their labours were rewarded and they had contributed in no small measure to a local masonic future.

What was it that they had produced? A place for 60 cars to park without any trouble and at no cost. A centre at no great distance from the main road leading south or north through the town or country. A building that had no neighbours and was devoid of noise and bustle. A masonic hall that could be, and by now has been, even further developed from what was then achieved. A place where, today, they do not need to dine out but can spend their whole evening in comfort and relaxation.

From the porchway or entrance one enters a vestibule leading to the main cloak and robing room with the added possibility of a smaller room for senior brethren or special guests from the Province. A staircase leads to an upper room to be used as a committee room and which could also be used, as it now is, for essential extra storage. On the right of the vestibule a new dining room has been finished which is panelled and decorated in a style to fit with the rest of the accommodation and at one end of this room a roomy bar can at last give the brethren the refreshments they need before and during the dinner.

It is now that we come to the surprise in what might otherwise be considered but a rather well-appointed but ordinary hall. You turn to the left and enter the temple through a lovely mahogany door with matching casings.

Before you stretches a lofty and spacious room 60 feet long and 30 feet wide. The walls are panelled with Burmese teak Bowgrain and the floor covered with Rhodesian Teak Feltwood, with a tesselated pavement in its appropriate position.

From the floor to the roof beams is some 21 feet. The bare trusses and rafters, thrown into relief by most cleverly concealed lighting and decoration, give a very refreshing sense of lightness and dignity, and turn what could so easily be just the skeleton of a shed into a place with atmosphere and character. You know that it *was* a cow shed; you know far more surely that it *is* a fascinating and memorable masonic lodge room. It may not have the aura yet of those halls in this volume that can plead a century or more of occupation and association. I can only say that having been to this hall on three separate occasions I am sensible of this place gaining constantly in quality. It is a hall that will be historic indeed in the years ahead.

Yet it is not just the framework of the hall or the practical fact that the raised dais in this room serves the dual purpose of providing better visibility for the rear seats and concealing the air ducting. It is that the hall has been graciously filled with items of masonic interest from De Tabley's own past elsewhere. A magnificent pair of globes on their stands catch the eye. A handsome banner from Provincial Grand Lodge which belonged to the late Lord de Tabley and was worked by his daughters. A glinting sacred symbol is suspended from the ceiling, and a hanging painted floor cloth, the work of Bro Brown of Chester and presented by Bro George Cornwall Legh MP. At meetings you would be struck by the 'costly and chaste set of jewels' also presented by the first WM, the poet Baron, and a silver collar chain of some 15 links and pendant presented by Bro Drucquer to mark his appreciation of being allowed to initiate his son in this lodge.

From 1863 there is a mahogany case with four dozen engraved glasses, whilst the ballot box of fine mahogany was given the next year. The collecting box for alms is pure silver and the tracing boards, though not exceptional, are already almost a century old. Indeed one could quite keep one's eyes on the floor of the lodge, and forget for a moment the work of restoration around, and it would be quite possible to see the De Tabley Lodge at work as it has been for its whole 125 years. It is this that is so memorable—the fine modern setting for a Craft lodge—and other degrees—that ever remind us of history and a past tradition.

If the reader should doubt these words of description I would like to cap them with some further words from the one whose generosity in the first place made all the subsequent work and outcome possible. Col Leicester-Warren wrote:

> The work which has been put in by so many members and the money that has been raised for the project must be an inspiration to all connected with it and demonstrates how worthwhile it has all been.

It isn't only the workers who can know that. Anyone who is fortunate enough to go as a visitor will come away with some inspiration as well.

LEICESTER

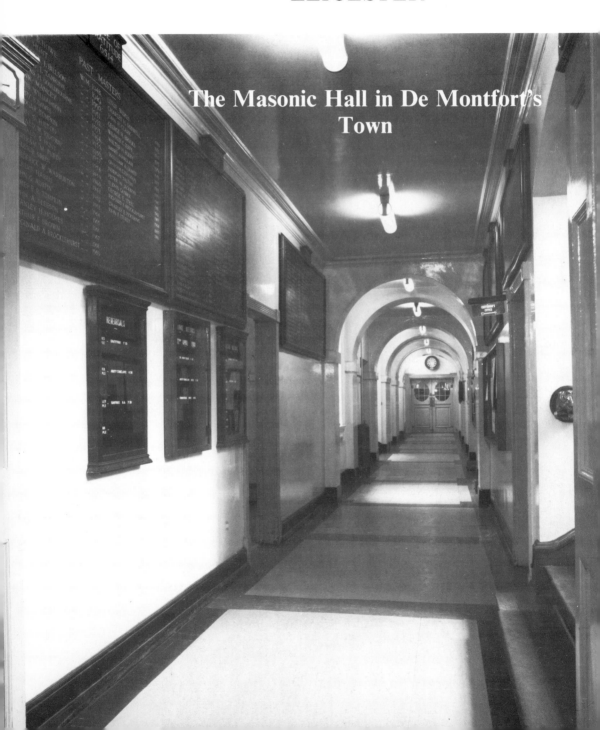

The Masonic Hall in De Montfort's Town

No-ONE WHO VISITS Leicester today can be in any doubt about its long and fascinating history. Its buildings give the clue. The centre of the modern city is the Clock Tower, a Victorian imitation Gothic monument near where the old East Gate stood. The town hall is handsome Renaissance while near Victoria Park is the De Montfort Hall, the city's principal meeting place for concerts and large gatherings. Abbey Park speaks of the building in which the notorious Cardinal Wolsey died, whilst St Nicholas' church has a Saxon nave, a Norman tower and is partly built of Roman materials. The whole city is an amalgam of rich and varied past and its freemasonry, though occupying the later centuries of this cavalcade, has its own fascinating story to tell and a memorable Masonic Hall to represent it to the brethren of today.

Freemasonry is known to have been practised in Leicestershire since the first half of the eighteenth century and there is proof of the existence of a lodge (No 170) in 1739. It met at the Wheat Sheaf inn which no longer exists, even as a site, and it was followed some 15 years later by the lodge meeting at the 'Pelican', Gallowtree Gate. The seals of yet another lodge in 1764 are preserved in the present Masonic Hall Museum, but both this and the others just mentioned all vanished leaving just one lodge, St John's, first of all No 562 (now No 279), with a warrant dated 1790, authorising them to meet at the sign of the Crown and Thistle, Loseby Lane.

It was under the auspices of St John's Lodge that we have the first record of a Leicestershire Provincial Grand Lodge, even though there has been a PGM since 1774. The Provincial Lodge met at the 'Lion and Dolphin' in the Market Place on 18 June 1793. It is noteworthy that the officer presiding over this meeting was the Revd W. Peters, Rector of Knipton, RA, who was not only the Grand Portrait Painter of the Craft but was also Provincial Grand Master of Lincolnshire. Indeed he held the post of Deputy PGM of Leicestershire and this other for 21 years though he can hardly have been overworked, for after the mention of the above meeting there is no extant record of any other Provincial gathering in Leicester until 1816. There were then only four more meetings up to 1833 and it was in the minutes of St John's Lodge alone that even a record of these has remained!

It is therefore no surprise to learn from the same record that it was in 1825 that there was the first, if abortive, attempt to erect a 'Freemasons Hall and Tavern' on a site extending from Market Street to Bowling Green Street. It 'visualised a building applicable for every public purpose, such as reading rooms, ball room,

The library and museum at Leicester contains one of the most extensive collections outside London.

concert room etc. and a Tavern upon a genteel and comfortable scale'. (One is reminded of the building taken over in Gt Yarmouth, see p151). Certainly this was thought to be too optimistic a venture for little enthusiasm was shown for its support and 17 more years were to elapse before a similar unsuccessful effort was suggested for Wycliff Street and Millstone Lane. Despite the fact that this venture was to cost only £1,200 as compared with the previous scheme of £4,000 it was also abandoned and meetings were held in the '3 Cranes' or 'The Bell'.

At last, in 1858, a third endeavour proved successful and a site in Halford Street soon saw a building erected on it at a cost of £3,500. Only 81 brethren were involved and finding the capital of £2,000 was no small undertaking. However, the corner stone was laid in February, 1859 by Rt Wor Bro Earl Howe and after a service at St George's Church in September the Provincial Grand Lodge assembled to dedicate the finished hall. The bethren of today might well raise their eyebrows at the idea of then incorporating a 'beerhouse' in the proposed plan, but this was in fact their intention and it is known to this day as 'The Coventry Arms'. A square and compasses still decorate the front of that building which is used as a normal public house.

The lodge room could be easily reached by either of the two staircases but in case that seems an advantage it was also the case that someone calling from the kitchen could be heard in the temple! It can be well imagined that tyling was a problem when those at labour could hear the summons 'to come to supper before the cook's efforts were ruined'. This upper chamber was heated by large open fireplaces and as it was 59 feet long and over 20 feet high it clearly needed them for much of the year. In the Holmes temple of today's hall can be seen some of the effects of this older centre. One can see the damage done by the heat to the oil painting of the Earl Howe which previously hung over one of the fireplaces, whilst three fine mahogany chairs, once the property of the John Gaunt Lodge, are also now in use there. Other items are found elsewhere in the present centre—the tracing boards which were laid on the centre of the black and white carpet are still in very good condition, which is as well for they are of unusual design, being painted on reinforced canvas stretched on wooden frames. They hang today on the walls of the Morley ante room.

In the Holmes temple one can also see the portrait of a Deputy Prov. Grand Master, Bro S. S. Partridge, to whom was handed the golden key for the new organ installed after 1903. When it was newly in place a concert was given to which the ladies were also invited. They would also have appreciated the refreshments which were prepared in the kitchens that had been extended after 1883. Yet even this kind of addition to the facilities was becoming inadequate, for what had been quite enough for two or three lodges at the outset was, by 1907, trying to cope with over 600 masons. More commodious premises were becoming an urgent necessity.

When a committee met in April of that year it was reported that the existing building was 'insanitary, uncomfortable, too small and lacking essential facilities'. At last a new one was recommended after looking at no less than 40 sites! It was the semi-detached and pleasing house at 80 London Road, standing on 1676 sq yards of land and it could be bought for £2500. It had been until recently the residence of Miss Needham. In his encouragement to back the scheme the Provincial Grand Treasurer of the day remarked 'that the members of the Province form a body of men strong enough to provide for their own needs and to

The Holmes temple with its magnificent ceiling

make provisions to meet the needs of those who will follow'. Yet there were strong words of disagreement from the WM of the Lodge 2429 who was 'entirely opposed to the scheme because we are purchasing a property without any money to pay for it and the site will deteriorate rather than improve in value'. His sincerity was never in question—but his judgement has been proved sadly awry.

When the brethren left Halford Street in 1909 they were able, after settling any outstanding mortgages, to hand over £3150 towards the new centre's cost of £12,500—which, in the light of subsequent developments, was an astonishing bargain! Happily they were able also to transfer the corner stone of the previous hall to London Road and it will now be seen on the Grand Staircase leading to the Holmes temple. The silver trowel and walnut setting maul used with it are also preserved in the museum. There are also further mementoes of the past in the present building—two old subscription boards recording amounts given by individuals, lodges and chapters to offset the mortgage at Halford Street. They are now on the main staircase leading to the Oliver temple. Here too the visitor can see photographs that show what a fine room for its day was the main lodge room. The fanlight, the delicate arcading, the fireplaces and the portraits, the flooring and the organ casing all made it in to a most pleasant meeting place.

Even to this day the frontage of the Leicester Masonic Hall, with its two pleasing late Georgian house elevations and porticoed entrance, belie the truly amazing arrangements which one finds on penetrating the building. This is even more the case since the still further extensions which were made at the rear in 1964, but from the start of the use of the premises it was clearly the intention to make this one of the finest masonic centres in the whole country. It can be said to have retained that objective and to have fulfilled many aspirations. It is a Masonic Hall which is indeed memorable.

The unusual and contrasting décor of the four temples, and not least the spacious, airy and tastefully furnished museum and library, may well be the envy of many a visiting brother. Over 500 brethren can be provided with dining accommodation and there is an extensive range of robing, committee and administrative rooms, not to mention the carefully organised kitchen arrangements. All this is provided behind what are house fronts that are 'listed' by the local authority and in well-maintained structures that would be a tribute to any properly conducted business concern.

The foundation stone of this great masonic 'home' is still clearly displayed with the silver trowel and ebony maul used by the Rt Hon the Earl Ferrers, encased on the wall above it and his portrait hanging above both. A year later the Pro Grand Master, the Rt Hon the Lord Ampthill, dedicated the hall in the presence of over 500 brethren. The first temple was later called 'Holmes' after the Provincial Grand Master who had reigned from 1913 to 1928. He was a masonic architect in a somewhat different sense in that when he was appointed the work done in the ceremonies was not at that level of dignity and sincerity which is now regularly expected. As the new PGM let it be known that he might visit without any notice and that trenchant and telling observations might be the result if needed, a singular change began to come over the presentation of degree ceremonies in the new headquarters, as elsewhere.

The order of architecture in this temple is Roman Ionic, the ceiling being in the form of a barrel arch divided into three sections by moulded ribs. In the centre of each section is a semi-circular space draped with crimson and gold damask and this again is interspersed with broad bands of fruit and flowers in high relief. There is more decoration of the same kind all around the outer rims of each square.

The ceiling itself is covered with emblems and designs, all in modelled relief and picked out in gold, silver and other colours. Its base colour is sky blue, representing the Canopy of Heaven, and in the centre section the seven-pointed star in gold has an all-seeing Eye at its heart and is surrounded by the constellation of the Great Bear and several minor ones. In the western section are the setting sun and other star clusters, whilst the moon and seven stars are in the eastern end. In each corner of the various sections are the 12 signs of the Zodiac which we have seen not infrequently in modern as well as much older masonic centres. (See the chapter on Stony Stratford, and also on Brighton in vol 1). There are also four tassels which represent the four cardinal virtues and these also we have seen elsewhere (see Faversham vol 1) and York (vol 3). The border round the base of the ceiling area is distinctive in showing Craft, Royal Arch, Mark and Royal Ark Mariner emblems, whilst the jewels of the officers of the Provincial Grand Lodge appear in the light blue, dark blue and red bands that separate each wall section. The impression that one already has of immense care in the design of this, the oldest lodge room here, and the rest of the room confirms that impression.

On either side of the organ gallery are two more ornamental panels. At the foot of each is the monogram of the Provincial Grand Lodge of Leicestershire and Rutland. Over this monogram is the circle with a point at its centre bounded by two parallel lines, representing, as we know, in original English masonry the two Saints John but later Moses and Solomon. On either side of these panels are sheaves of corn, whilst over the organ pipes, in a coffin-shaped panel are the emblems of mortality.

The east wall is panelled in mahogany, with a bold representation of the rising sun above, with a letter 'G' superimposed and an all-seeing eye at the latter's centre. Sheaves and ears of corn support the device and above it stands that reminder of time's march, the hour-glass. Once more the emblems of mortality lie at its foot. Over the Master's chair (as indeed on the old Provincial banner) there is an illuminated representation of the Grand Lodge coat of arms—a practice not now countenanced by that body. Most distinctive here are the two human faces on either side of the canopy over the Master's place—one has the eyes closed and the other open, thus reminding us of the candidate before and after his initiation. The same motif is repeated on the bronze lighting brackets at the side of the doors in the west.

Twelve green marbled pillars give the appearance of supporting the barrel roof. Between them, and on the canvas covered walls, are twelve portraits in oil of past PGMs, Deputy PGMs and Grand Superintendents, each individually illuminated. Some of those whose likenesses hang here have already been mentioned.

To reach this very delightful Holmes temple the visitor will have entered from the street, passed along the processional corridor straight ahead of him and then taken a gentle winding flight of marble stairs to the right to reach the same kind of corridor on the floor above. This leads via one more flight of stairs to the Holmes room. Yet, in making our way there and just before the second lot of stairs, we should pause for a moment to look into the most excellent library in this building. It is, with justice, claimed to be the finest such library and museum outside that in

The Holmes temple looking west with the organ gallery and adjacent panels.

Great Queen Street, London. Housed in spacious glass-fronted mahogany cases will be found a large number of rare and valuable volumes on English and foreign Freemasonry. Apart from all the usual histories, year books, lodge booklets and collections of Research Transactions there is a very wide and well-catalogued collection of other books on many allied subjects. Old rituals, copies of exposures and manuscript versions of the ceremonial are all tabulated, and alongside these verbal reminders of the past there are also certificates, coins, pieces of unusual regalia, pictures, jewels, seals, stained glass, china and objets d'art—all of absorbing interest to any mason who wishes to promote his knowledge. It is also worth noting that there are some old swords, stone-laying tools, a scale model of King Solomon's Temple and some very interesting local playhouse bills showing local masonic support and patronage.

Here too will be found the famous Thorp collection with its own beautiful and rare jewels, its well-collected books and works of reference. Bro J. T. Thorp, whose portrait hangs on the main stairway leading to the next major Temple, that named after Col Oliver, was the Founder and first Master of the Lodge of Research, No 2429. He was also the editor for many years of the Transactions of that lodge which still greatly flourishes, as well as curator and librarian of this hall's library. This much cherished collection was bequeathed in 1932.

As we pass along the corridors of this fine masonic hall we shall notice, among the usual lists of past masters and principals, one special board showing those brethren who have occupied the position of Mayor, or Lord Mayor, of Leicester. It is a most telling record. Other unusual wall decorations are the complete range of painted lodge crests that adorn the walls of the Holmes' suite dining room.

It was in 1935 that the demand for space, even in what was then a large hall, required the purchase of No 78 London Road and the erection of another sizeable temple and its dining room, a new robing room, four more committee rooms and enlarged kitchen facilities. The new committee rooms have their own particular charm and some of them have the most lovely furniture. Tables, chairs, desks and mirrors have been selected and placed with a real sense of style.

Retracing our steps, but turning right before reaching the main stairs we come by another pair of rising flights to the door of the ante-room and preparation room leading to the Oliver temple. The walls of the ante-room are covered in bold, embossed, red and gold flock paper, and it is here that one can see the old Provincial banner which was in use from 1880 to 1953.

This temple does not have any distinctive architectural style as it was designed for use by other than Craft bodies, as well as the usual lodges and chapters. The ceiling is flat, being broken up into a series of sky blue rectangular sections with moulded roof beams between them and these beams painted magnolia but picked out in red and gold. All around the room and just below the ceiling border are a number of recessed and illuminated panels in which are the coloured reliefs of the collars of distinguished officers—the Grand Master, the Provincial and Deputy Provincial GMs, Grand Superintendent, etc. Crests of the current PGM and the Province are over the dais in the east whilst in the west are those of the past PGMs and the three Masonic Institutions and the Hospital.

The walls are divided into a series of panels by marbled pilasters of classical design, and the panels are decorated to give the effect of draped green and gold cloth falling to about 3 feet from the floor. Over the doorway, which simulates black-veined marble with scarlet and gold ornament, there is depicted a setting sun in gold. The electric organ, which was the gift of Bro F Pollard, gains its power from a valve chamber behind the lovely Australian walnut panelling in the east. The central portion is marked by a pentagram on which is superimposed a letter G with an all-seeing eye again at its centre. Some folding screens can be drawn across this temple to divide it up for other purposes.

RW Bro Colonel Sir Frederick Oliver died at the outbreak of war in 1939 and was succeeded by Sir John Corah. An emergency temple of more modest dimensions was already in existence when, in 1960, just after Sir John's resignation, it was further enlarged to accommodate 50 brethren and was re-furnished. Its walls are covered with delicate grey canvas, its ceiling blue and its west end panelled in mahogany with ebony bandings. The usual but smaller black and white carpet rests on a matching grey one. Happily, Sir John Corah was able to be present when this temple, often used by smaller and newer lodges, was dedicated in his name. His personal standard has been placed in a permanent position above the Junior Warden's chair and thus keeps a lasting link with this PGM who maintained the Province through the testing war and post-war years.

A tasteful committee room.

When Col Oliver was dedicating the temple with his name he remarked that '...
we have built this extension with an eye to our future development and for the
comfort of the generations who will follow'. It was almost the same sentiments as
that expressed thirty years before and such as was to be repeated thirty years
afterwards. For now, on the next floor above and yet alongside the area of the
Oliver temple, there is a third and even more ample room with very impressive
seating. With still more modern lines and lighting, but built to meet a new
generation of masons and the needs of over 65 lodges in this part of the Province, it
makes a yet further addition to that list of remarkable premises that lie behind
what is still a most attractive and quite modest hall entrance. No-one who takes
the trouble to pause in his journeys and enter through those two slender pillars and
up the five steps can be anything but rewarded by his masonic visit here. He will
indeed have encountered a truly memorable masonic hall.

The main staircase with lodge boards kept in pristine condition.

LETCHWORTH

The Lodge Room in the Cloisters

BETWEEN NOVEMBER 1905 and November 1907 a certain Miss A. J. Lawrence
founded in Hertfordshire a School of Psychology which had as its principal object
the study of 'how thought affects action and what causes and produces thought.'
The school was to be situated in the buildings at Letchworth Garden City called
'The Cloisters' and at the Opening Ceremony on 28 January, 1907, Miss Lawrence
made the following dedication:

> To the Unity, Eternal Reality, through all diverse, temporary and fragmentary
> seemings, the perfect inviolable whole, wherein sin and pain and death are not,
> and all contradictions are reconciled, all discords resolved, I dedicate this
> building, confident that, through progressive recognition of this unity, mankind
> will ascend to a full, harmonious and joyful expression of life, in soul, body and
> social organisation.

It was to be a singularly apt statement in view of the later use made of the Cloisters
by the freemasons.

Meanwhile the building was constructed on very definite and intentionally
symbolic patterns. The Swedish green marble columns set around the cloister
garth in pairs were specially chosen and cut so as to show the veining running
vertically to give a strong idea of upward growth and aspiration. The green
colouring of these columns is carried up in the form of mosaic into the arches, and
has a high polish after the manner of holly leaves.

A change in the marble was made to red Ipplepen for the two open fireplaces
and this was carried up into the arches where it was to intermingle with the green,
the idea being that the fires have changed the green to red marble.

At the dedication an inscription, written and illuminated on vellum by the
architect, was enclosed in a glass casket, and placed in the cavity made in the
springer stone over the fountain in the entrance hall. It was then sealed with a
small stone cap.

From below this cap crystal streams of water were meant to flow in symbolism
of the purest and fundamental motives for erecting the building. This water was to
fall into the upper basin of the fountain, and then run away at the foot in an
emblematical way across the cloister. Meanwhile the lower basin to the fountain is
a 'lavabo' with eight small basins with hot and cold water supplied to provide
handwashing for the guests. The small hooks above the basins were for cups. This
ingenious feature is the one that meets the masonic visitor today as he enters the

building. It may not function but its original purpose is clear and it certainly forms a most unusual introduction to a masonic hall.

The variety of the texture of this building is certainly one of its most memorable features. The foundations of the building and the basement walls are built of blue lias lime concrete, the facing bricks are hand-made creamy bricks from Suffolk and all the stone is Purbeck stone quarried near Swanage, Dorset, and chosen on account of the variety of tints it shows. Creamy pink tiles were used for the jambs and mullions of the bay windows whilst red tiles were used for the roofs. The effect, even today and after many alterations have been made to enclose the building and make it suitable for all masonic uses, is of a meeting place that is unique and distinctive.

Following the original plan a very fine four-manual electric organ was installed in a recess of the main hall and this was to have an echo organ in a chamber specially selected. The shape of the building gives unusually fine acoustic results as indeed anyone who tries them out today will soon discover.

Finally, the glazing of the three upper tiers of casements in the southwest alcove and the south windows in the cloisters proper was only meant to be temporary. In

The cloisters at Letchworth, once a school! of Psychology now a masonic hall.

due time it was intended that there would be stained glass with a scheme portraying the rising and setting of the sun. Sadly this was never done but one can see that it would have had a special significance for the property's eventual occupiers if it had been so completed.

Writing about the work that was being done in this remarkable building in 1908 one magazine contributor had this to say:

> It is hoped that there may in time go forth from this centre a number of strong and joyous men, experienced in wholesome thought and labour, to preach and practise among the masses of the people a wholesome emancipating gospel and saner mode of living.

With only slight adjustment to the latter phrasing the objectives suggested could be no less fittingly applied to the Hertfordshire brethren whose meetings were in due time to replace those of the eager young students whom Miss Lawrence was so keen to encourage.

Again, shortly afterwards, a well-known American journalist wrote as follows:

> The Cloisters, though named a school, would be more accurately called a Temple—dedicated to the Perfect Life. We live in a period of transition. We have known the faith of our forefathers constantly repudiated. We have shared in that repudiation. And there is growing up amongst us a broader, grander, nobler faith, which embraces all human kind, all that lives indeed, and holds it to be One. See how far this idea of Unity leads those who believe . . . that which harms our brother harms us and what he has not, that do we also lack. And so this 20th century Temple is erected to the hallowing of humanity.

That, by no stretch of the imagination, was an observation that we might hope would be made now when the occupants are our fellow brethren in the Craft.

It remains only to allow David Garnett, the author and nephew of the architect, to paint for us the kind of life which was being spent here in the year 1910. This at least is different from any masonic activity!

> One slept in a canvas cot, swinging a couple of feet off the floor, sheltered from the rain or snow, but in the open. In the morning one hauled up one's bed, either had a hot bath or a plunge in the swimming pool, collected a breakfast, which was eaten sitting raised up behind a vast slab of rose-coloured alabaster. The inter-locking windows of the cloister arches patterned the floor, and shafts of sunlight fell from the roof through its open louvres. Those breakfasting at the table looked like a painting of the Last Supper.

Such was the idyllic life which those who came to the Cloisters were expecting if not always practising and which was maintained for the first quarter of the century up to the year before the Second World War. The Letchworth that Miss Lawrence first knew had grown from being a village to a town of over 15000 people and she was fast succumbing to deafness and other bodily weaknesses. The desires she had hoped to foster and develop were, however, still summed up in a verse she had recited at the last residential course here:

When each to all shall be a brother,
  Not 'Help yourself', but 'Help each other',
The highest state of man be reached
  When he lives as the Master preached.

That is surely a good note on which to turn to the apparent speedy decision by
Miss Lawrence to offer the building to the freemasons of Letchworth. The decision
is all the more understandable when one adds to her own physical deterioration
the state of the Cloisters at the time, the complete disappearance of all the fine
ideals and traditions of the work done there and the fact that in 1953 there had
been permission for the buildings to be transferred for use from a store for the
British Tabulating Company to a dancing academy. How the glory seems to have
departed!

The invitation to the freemasons seems to have come as a result of a chance
remark by a Mr Bainbridge during one of this routine visits to Miss Lawrence who
was by then permanently at St Catherine's Nursing Home. Once the offer had been
made to Miss Lawrence she was very anxious for it to be accepted and the whole
business to be settled as quickly as possible. That was in March 1948.

A confidential meeting was held with representatives from lodges and chapters

*The main temple at Letchworth with stoves at the base of the columns on the left and right and
the bricked-in arcades.*

in North Hertfordshire at which Lord Pethick Lawrence, the benefactor's brother, was also able to speak, and by 22 May after the whole proposal had been fully explained to a full meeting of masonic delegates Miss Lawrence's offer was received with sincere gratitude.

What was included in the gift was as follows—

The whole of the leasehold interest in the Cloisters, including the two cottages and Ladybarn, plus some other War Department compensation money *and* £100 pa for the remainder of her lifetime towards the upkeep of the building. At her death Miss Lawrence was arranging for the remainder of her estate to be paid over to the freemasons: a sum of about ten to fifteen thousand pounds.

Mr Pratt, the Surveyor to the First Garden City Ltd had been very anxious about how the premises would eventually be disposed of but when he heard that such a body as the freemasons were to take over the property he was sure that his Company would grant the necessary license for them to use it 'for such purposes as the Freemasons would reasonably require'.

Permission to change the use being thus likely it only remained to draw up the Memorandum and Articles for the new Trust Company and to raise the extra money needed to accomplish all the alterations that would be required in the structure. In November 1948 the Provincial Grand Master and some of his officers inspected the building and discussed the plans for the adaptation and modification of the Cloisters. They expressed their great interest in and approval for the whole project.

In June 1950 the Maintenance Committee had put in hand the work of filling in the spaces between the marble columns of the Cloister Garth to form the temple, the in-filling, to be around the outer edge of the outside pillars, of buff-coloured standard-sized bricks and the entrance doors of wood marked 'Yang'. It was also decided to remove the glazed doors at the south end leading into the garden and build a temporary wall in their place. The remains of the organ were sold and with some scrap metal from the fittings on the fountain and the cleats for drawing up the hammock beds went to Letchworth Casting Co who smelted them down and recast the metal to make a plaque which would commemorate the gift of the Cloisters. The second initiate to the Cloisters Lodge presented this to the Trust in January 1952. It read:

"You have made good work
You and your apron men."
Coriolanus, iv, 6,
THIS PLAQUE COMMEMORATES THE GIFT OF THE CLOISTERS
BY
Miss A. J. LAWRENCE
to
THE FREEMASONS OF LETCHWORTH, BALDOCK AND DISTRICT
5th April 1949
"I will as 'twere a brother of your order
Visit both prince and people".
Measure for Measure, 1.4.

Within the next two years the Trust had spent over £3,500 on repairs and alterations. Before the first masonic meeting, that of the Cloisters Lodge, was held there in October 1951 the temple had been extended to enable 200 brethren to assemble in comfort and an electronic organ had been purchased from Millers of Norwich. Thus the building was in use as a masonic centre before Miss Lawrence passed away though sadly she was never well enough to be able to make the journey to see what had been done to her Cloisters.

By 1954 the Trust could report that the income was larger than expenditure, that chairs for use in the temple had been presented by a number of brethren and that the condition of the marble pillars at the entrance were in such a state as to warrant the attention of a monumental mason. This work, like the work first done at the porchway of King Solomon's Temple, proved to be very costly indeed.

In 1955, WBro Bainbridge, the first instigator of this transfer to the freemasons, offered to improve at his own expense the east end of the temple by building a recess for the Master's chair and his offer was gratefully accepted. The result is today very clear.

Slowly but surely the Cloisters began to take shape in their new guise but the lack of a dining room was a serious drawback to the smooth running of lodge meetings since the temple had to be cleared up at the end of its meeting so that the tables for supper could be laid up for the meal to begin. This became even more evident when by January 1958 two more Craft lodges, a Royal Arch Chapter, a Mark and Royal Ark Mariner lodges and a Knight Templar preceptory all began to attend here. In 1959 this need was at last met and on 18 November there was a dedication of the temple alterations and the opening of the dining hall. These together cost £8000.

Meanwhile the Cecil Lodge offered its delightful furniture for permanent use in the main temple and the acceptance of this enabled two lodges of instruction rooms to be equipped for masonic work. The same lodge, being the owners of a lodge carpet recently presented by the Brothers Russell and having no immediate use for it, offered it to the Trust for use in the temple. It was extended to a length of thirteen yards at a cost of £55 and today graces the floor of the temple here. Following this generous lead the Baldock Lodge also made a present of their furniture for use in one of the new instruction rooms.

To finish off the extensions and changes made there was, on 17 September 1967, a very memorable ceremony. Mrs K. Bainbridge, in the presence of a large number of brethren and their wives, duly opened the "The T. B. Bainbridge Room" to commemorate the immense debt of all the brethren whose masonic home is now the Cloisters to this kindly man who had brought about this establishment and then proceeded to donate to its development from his own means. With that new LOI room the building became what we see today.

Here is a hall that does not have the patina of age that we may see in other buildings mentioned in this collection. Yet there can be no doubt in the mind of any visitor to Letchworth that this is indeed a memorable building. As we reflect on its past and consider the strange but providential connection between its first conception and the present usage one cannot be other than impressed with the wonderful way in which this is still becoming a masonic home of distinction. As you pause to admire the entrance-hall fountain, wander along the now enclosed cloister way, admire the unusual features of the temple itself (and especially the

now adapted fireplaces and bricked-up arches), and finally seat yourself in the
ample dining room with its architectural features that make it so unusual you
cannot but admire those who have passed this way before and made this a hall to
remember.

In the cloisters themselves you will find a lovely coloured print of the finished
Temple at Jerusalem with its walls, towers and sanctuary all complete, shining in
the sun and dominating the great mount of Moriah. Passing from it are the
pilgrims or visitors who have tasted its wonder and shared in its ceremonies. As I
left that hall for the first time I was strangely like them. Impressed and intrigued by
what my brothers had accomplished to the honour of the GAOTU.

LUDLOW

The Masonic Hall in an Ancient Marcher Town

THE SILURES, WE are told, were a powerful and warlike tribe of ancient Britons who offered a fierce resistance to the Roman occupation (between 48 and 78 AD) in the border country between England and Wales. It might, therefore, have seemed only right that in 1791 there should be erected at Kington, Herefordshire, a masonic lodge bearing the name of Silurian. What battle and conflict might not have gained, brotherly love was eventually to establish. It was also to influence freemasonry in the old Roman camp site that is now called 'The hill by the swift-flowing stream'—Ludlow.

The lodge was actually warranted by that ubiquitous Provincial Grand Master in so many shires, Thomas Dunckerley, but though it was intended by warrant to meet at the Sun Inn as the second lodge in the Province it is sadly to be reported that the sun did not shine on it for long as the last mention of its members on the Grand Lodge Register is in 1796 and by 1800 it was on the point of extinction. The cash remaining was divided amongst the brethren who remained and by 1804 the furniture including the jewels, had been sold by the Treasurer to a person in Ludlow for the sum of £22 10s 0d. It was not sold without a purpose for in 1805 a new lodge in the town was formed, only this time bearing a Saxon name from across the border—the Mercian Lodge, No 528. Whether it had been planned or no the fact is that the items that had been sold passed immediately into the possession of Mercian and the warrant of the defunct lodge was also transferred to it. Indeed, if you look around the present Masonic Hall in Ludlow, which we are about to visit, you will still see that ancient warrant proudly displayed, and bearing the necessary endorsement of 1805.

The two lodges, however, did not only share the same warrant and furniture but even the residue of the membership for there was at least one brother, the Revd John Thomas, of Lucton, who belonged to both. The lodge was to meet at the Angel Inn and did so for the first time on 7 May, 1806, when the first Master was John Beebee Morris (*sic*). He was either an exceptional Master or else kept off all other contenders for he occupied the chair for 14 consecutive years! When he gave up the office he was presented with a PM's jewel made of old paste and silver, which we know because that item too is still in the present hall's collection. At the Union the lodge actually shared one more thing with Silurian for it was given exactly the same number, 528.

Another treasured possession in the hall at Ludlow is a book given to the Mercian Lodge by Bro Edward Wellings in 1805. The first three pages contain

some very fine pen and ink drawings of masonic subjects and they are followed by
a transcript of the 24 bye-laws made on 7 May that year. The book becomes even
more precious by having the actual signatures of various brethren in what is
otherwise a but little known masonic unit. By 1815 the lodge number was 485 as
confirmed on an old tobacco box which is still preserved. From Grand Lodge
records we know that the lodge worked for about 20 years, with its last initiation in
1821, its last contribution to Grand Lodge funds in 1826, and its actual dissolution
in 1828, though it was 1832 before it was erased at the further re-numbering of the
lodges.

What is somewhat surprising is that its members continued to survive despite
what seems like a total blank in Ludlow's masonic life. Even in 1853 there were
still 4 members of Mercian alive—Bros Anderson, Griffiths, Urwick and Whittall.
Indeed, it was on the authority of Bro G Anderson, as late as 1864, that the entry
was made in the Wellings book mentioned above to the effect that it *was* 1828
when the Mercian lodge was actually dissolved. It was certainly through the
instrumentality of these brethren that the warrant of Silurian, the jewels, the
furniture and the memory of the earlier lodges were assumed by the new and
continuing Lodge of the Marches, then No 887, which was warranted on 28
February, 1853. The new lodge met at the Golden Lion Hotel in the town when a
dispensation from Watkin Williams Wynn, Provincial Grand Master for Shropshire and North Wales, was issued to James Bach, Esq, WM Elect. The
dispensation reads strangely to our ears:

> 'I do hereby issue this my dispensation for such Lodge to meet and to proceed to
> work ... until the same shall be regularly Installed with its officers and
> constituted according to ancient custom.'

How, one might be tempted to ask today, could a lodge do any work without
knowing who its officers were? Was it in fact the case that those senior brothers
from Mercian days guided the Master Elect and newer brethren who had been
initiated elsewhere into procedures of which they still had a vivid memory?
Certainly the minutes confirm such a possibility for it was decided at the first
meeting that 'the surviving members of the Mercian Lodge shall be admitted as
members of the present lodge on payment of Grand Lodge dues only'.

The consecration duly took place on 13 June, 1853, and is worth remembering.
The Provincial Grand Master arrived by special train with his officers 'amidst the
firing of cannon, and the ringing of the bells of St Laurence Church'. The ensuing
banquet was also of note as there were 20 toasts with music after each one.

The lodge had several meeting places in the town and at one time even met in the
Old Rectory. The number of the lodge as it is at present, No 611, was granted in
1862 and the badge of the lodge was formalised with the names of Silurian and
Mercian incorporated in the title. By 1884 the members had had enough trouble
with meeting places and were determined to find a more permanent home. They
obtained some premises in Brand Lane adjoining the site of the present Hall and
by free loans, some borrowing and a balance from the lodge funds, they were at
last in possession of a property. The lodge certainly seems at this stage to have
taken on new heart for at the Provincial Grand Lodge in Shrewsbury in October
1885 there were present 21 members of the total of 32 on the lodge register.

This may not seem to be confirmed by the minutes of a meeting in 1885 when only 3 members and one visitor were recorded as present—but then it was the occasion of the last General Election at which Ludlow had the right to elect an MP. The brethren may have been exhorted, as now, to keep politics from the lodge room but they obviously felt strongly about being at the hustings in their private capacities.

The lodge continued to be active and to develop its own distinctive ways. In 1900 a candidate for Passing recited not only the answers to the questions showing his proficiency but also the G and S Ob which he took as an entered apprentice. From that time to the present the same practice is required of all other candidates in order to emphasise the responsibilities which each brother owes to the Craft.

Before the Jubilee year of 1903 the lodge was freed from debt and plans could be made to further improve the premises. They were able to purchase the adjoining property for £325 and on this being demolished the present temple, a large and lofty square room, was erected at a further cost of £600. This meant that the old temple could become the dining room, but whilst this was obviously a real step forward the change put an end to a constant tradition of the lodge from its inception. The custom of drinking the health of the newly-installed Master during the inner working was no longer permitted. Grand Lodge had decreed in 1902 that henceforth no liquor was to be allowed in temples. The brethren of 'The Marches'

The Master's place at Ludlow: notice the position of the ashlars on the chequered pavement.

could toast the Master, as we all do, at dinner but a little bit of (Mercian?) tradition was at last lost.

Further improvements to the hall were to follow as part of the Jubilee. The oak panelling of the temple was carried out in 1913 and the three chairs already in the lodge's possession were matched by 24 more of the same design. By 1922 the loans taken out to finance the changes were all paid and a chequered flooring was now laid. New lodges now sprang from the mother lodge of the Marches ... Teme, Longmynd and Cleobury.

The actual hall to which we must now turn our attention has been well described by the lodge historian, on the occasion of the 125th anniversary of the lodge, as combining 'character, tradition and charm; it attracts the envy of many who come to visit us; it is a building and headquarters of which we are justly proud ...' It stands in one of the connecting streets of the lower part of the town (Brand Lane) and though it has been looked for it leaves one in no doubt as to its purpose when at last you stand before it. It has a pale blue gable-end façade pierced by a white pillared and elegantly decorated doorway with a triangular pediment above it, and two similarly designed windows flanking it. Above these is a tall arched white window, with a definite keystone and heavy white base and it might well be guessed that those who care for buildings have a care for this early nineteenth century property. To leave the visitor in no doubt, however, the base of the upper window is also flanked by two white stone squares, that on the left bearing a square and compasses, and that on the right showing a pentagram. Below these figures are the words, in large blue capitals, MASONIC HALL.

The clear division of the earlier building, and the annexe which was later acquired, can be seen by the total difference of outside frontage to the right as you face it where a flat-topped structure with three pilasters and two large arcades adorn a sombre brownstone wall. It is behind this part of the building that the main temple lies and it is, of course, reached by entering the old hallway 'next door' and passing through the ante-room to the right with its red carpet and pleasant décor., The room you then enter has the air of being occupied much longer than has in fact been the case and this sense of history is no doubt enhanced by the presence of those items of furniture and decoration which relate to the story of local masonry which has been recounted.

Panelled in mahogany the three principal chairs incorporate the original furniture of 1791 but also show that the materials then used were of earlier ecclesiastical origin. Tall and upright as they are, with crosses on the back rest and footrests added later, they have a simple dignity in this lofty temple. The matching Chippendale candlesticks, each of a different order of architecture and with steps at the base covered in a chequered style, also add to the scene, and they are complemented by two delightful globes in their brass holders, though in this case they are unusually placed on delicate pillars which very closely resemble the smaller candleholders. These pillars were purchased from the Royal Edward Lodge at Leominster and presented to this lodge in 1970. They were in a state of dilapidation, having been stored in a room with a leaking roof. The globes are by Newton and Berry and dated 1839 and, as we have found in the case of Worksop (see p144) the names on the terrestrial globe are well worth study. The pillars originated as large altar candlesticks, and are probably also Chippendale.

The room is well endowed with many more carved oak chairs of fascinating designs and, with the two name boards behind them illustrating the already long list of Masters, one can again appreciate why this temple produces a real sense of tradition. The new lodge banner from 1972 also has its own contribution of colour to make. The original Silurean warrant on the walls adds its own special mark.

What would strike a visitor who had the pleasure of being at a meeting in this hall is that even the jewels worn by the principal officers are also relics of the Silurean Lodge and date from 1791. The Master's jewel shows not only the usual square but has a charming little sun motif at the inner angle, and the Secretary's pens are beautifully fashioned quills tied with a rich knot. All the jewels are pure silver and are, I can testify, a delight to handle as well as to see.

One of the pleasures of this hall is that there are other items in the building which make it the memorable place it is. This is particularly the case in the present dining room which was, let us remember, for nearly twenty years the original temple. It is here that we see the old banner framed and it is not at all surprising that the local brethren took steps in 1970 to renovate the display cabinets in this room so that the other proud possessions could be properly seen and preserved. As was then found there had been a good deal of neglect in both recognising and protecting masonic items of some individuality and today the visitor can enjoy these in their well-arranged cases.

The temple, west end.

The principal cabinet contains some 30 items of which an ormolu clock of c1840 with masonic markings on the scroll, two volumes of the notable work, *Architectura* by Palladio, 3rd edition and with a preface by Inigo Jones and dated 1742, and two Sunderland jugs of c1805 with the punchbowl and ladles used in that old toasting ceremony of the Installed Masters board, are just a little taste of its contents. There is a fine array of glassware in the room, especially a beautifully cut glass Ale jug and a personal glass tankard belonging to one, Bro Lavender, whose name is thereon inscribed. It is thought that he may have been a retired lodge Tyler.

On the walls one can also see a framed set of Rose Croix regalia from the mid-nineteenth century, which is in very frail condition and has just been rescued in time. The same is true for the regalia of the Provincial Grand Master for Herefordshire in 1850 which was found in a cupboard, framed but with the glass broken and covered with damp mould. It was lovingly restored and cleaned and done so well that it could be worn today with grace on any occasion. The one jewel, in another frame, that catches the eye is the large one of a PM that was presented to WBro John Beebee Morris, the long-serving Master who was also an attorney.

Yet the two most fascinating and distinctive items here are the Brother Hixon apron and the original Silurean floor cloth/tracing board which has been called 'unique in the British Isles'. The apron comes from 1791 and is made of pure lambskin. It features the usual figures of Charity on the flap, Faith and Hope on the ends of a three-stepped platform with the former still holding a cross to emphasise the Christian nature of the Craft at this date. The centre is a rich medley of Bible, sun, moon, stars, ladder, candles, tools and ashlars—a veritable storehouse of teaching aids for the eager masonic student and an example of what was much more common once, for an identical apron can be seen in the Grand Lodge Museum of London.

The floor cloth, now so superbly displayed on the dining room wall, was recovered from a shelf in the ante-room where it had lain, forgotten and torn, for decades. It was expertly restored in 1969 on the advice of the curator of the Grand Lodge museum who was able to confirm that whilst it came from Silurean's heritage it was almost certainly older still. The cloth is about six feet long and two feet wide, with an indented border all round. Three steps in the foreground lead to an expanse of chequered flooring (in perspective) and at the end there stands, vertically, a tracing board with a representation of the Euclid Proposition which is being completed by a clothed wrist and hand holding a pencil. This board immediately suggests those similar small drawing boards which are seen in Lewes and Taunton (see the volume covering the South of England).

Flanking the board with the hand are the level and plumbrule, with a magnificent G and rays of light above them, whilst at the very head of the cloth is an open square with the arms pointing downwards to a rough ashlar on the left and a smooth one on the right. Here we are indeed in ancient English freemasonry and certainly no other hall so far visited has a cloth of this design or in quite this pristine condition. It is rightly regarded with pride and whilst we know that the toast to 'absent brethren' is really for those present-day masons who are not able to attend on any one evening I am sure that those who dine in this room today are helped to recall their brethren of nearly two centuries ago by looking upon this cloth as they eat.

Here then, is a hall not to be missed. In an ancient town that has its own very real treasures and pleasures it is especially good to know that the Masons of today know what a gem they possess. Whilst it is never fully possible to convey the 'feel' of a building without actually standing in it one hopes that what has been described will result in some masonic travellers pausing for a time on the Border and looking in at Brand Lane. The members of 611 want it known that they will always be pleased to see interested freemasons and to conduct them around their 'treasures'. Visitors will not be disappointed.

NORWICH

The Masonic Hall in St Giles Street

As you make your way from the ancient market place of this East Anglian capital
to the Roman Catholic cathedral you will come to the impressive masonic hall
which lies on your right hand side. Most striking are the six tall columns that grace
the first-floor façade. They separate five large sash windows each with their
triangular pediments above, and the indented cornice again above them, supporting a huge stone triangle with an enfoliated shield at its centre bearing the square
and compasses in the fellowcraft position. Below the centre window of the first
floor one's eye is then drawn to the huge porticoed doorway, its pillars braced with
rusticated blocks— as with all the window frames on the ground floor—and the
fanlight over the double blue doors being framed by a series of keystones under a
heavy cornice flanked by two broken segments of an unfinished arch, beneath
which stands a curved stone pedestal symbolising. . . . One is left with certain ideas.

This fine building has, of course, been the product of a long and steady history
of occupation. The need for such a centre was made clear as early as 1771 when a
letter to the Grand Secretary in London states:

> The Brethren at Norwich are very frequently removing from one Lodge to
> another, and when any one is weak, in order to assist it . . .

This movement of men was almost as frequently paralleled by the movement of
meeting places. The Perserverance Lodge started in the Turkey Cock in 1795 and
in the following 75 years it changed venue 18 times. It finished up in 1872 at the
Norfolk Hotel, St Giles Street, but only for a year and then moved 4 more times in
as many more years.

On 14 November, 1876, a lodge of Emergency was held at the Lamb Hotel,
when it was announced that as the premises in which they were then accustomed to
meet had been sold, and were about to be turned into a High School for Girls, they
would have to find other accommodation.

By 1879 the question of moving again was raised and this time the officers
agreed to move to No 23 (now the present 47) St Giles' Street, for the house there
had been taken as a masonic club. The site of the present hall, therefore, is now
able to record over a century of constant masonic occupation. The old local lodge
meeting there is Union, No 52.

The Norwich Masonic Association Ltd was formed with the express purpose of
providing a common meeting place for all the Norwich lodges. The shares were
subscribed for by Provincial Grand Lodge, by the individual lodges and by sundry
individual brethren. Transfers of the shares were restricted henceforth to masons

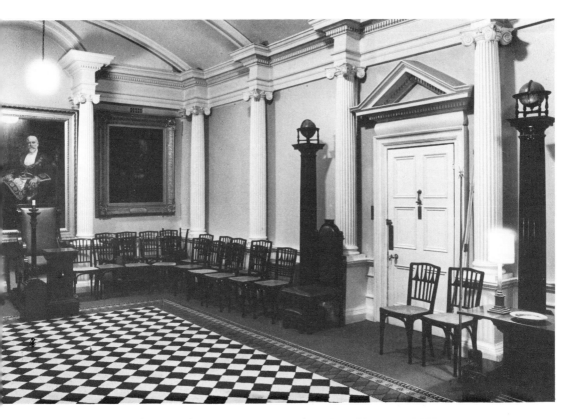

Le Strange temple looking towards the west. The portrait is of Hamon Le Strange who was Provincial Grand Master in 1906 when he dedicated the temple in his own name.

The imposing facade of Norwich Masonic Hall.

only. Perserverance Lodge held its first meeting there on 21 October and by the 14 November Cabbell and Sincerity lodges had followed suit. Union was to follow in 1887 when the hotel where they met underwent extensive alteration. The Social and Walpole Lodges made up the remainder of the complement there.

On 2 February, 1906, the growing pressure of lodges and their members meeting at the St Giles premises required the opening of a new temple and in the presence of some 100 brethren the RW Provincial Grand Master dedicated it in his own name — it is the 'Le Strange Temple' of today. A portrait of this very vigorous and ardent Norwich mason is also hanging in the present hall. It was first painted by Charles E. Butler and was presented when the Provincial Grand Lodge met at Fakenham in 1907. It is also worth noting that this brother was initiated in Apollo (Oxford University) lodge No 357, in 1861, became Master of Westminster and Keystone Lodge No 10 in 1873, was Master of Quatuor Coronati Lodge in 1906, wrote a most valuable history of the Province, and died, after 57 years of masonic service, in 1918. It is only right that such a leader in Norwich and its county should still be so remembered in the Provincial headquarters.

It was in 1922, at a meeting of the Provincial Grand Lodge in the local Grammar School, that the resolution was passed: 'That 20 guineas be set aside to form a nucleus of a fund to be called the Norfolk Masonic Building Fund for the purpose of providing better accommodation for the Provincial Grand Lodge and the lodges desiring to use the same'. A year later a Provincial Building Committee was set up with a member from each of the Norwich lodges to consider in more detail the matter of improving further the arrangements of the premises at 47 St Giles Street. As if to emphasise the point a St Giles lodge was consecrated in Norwich the same year, and the sense of unity amongst the Norwich brethren was shown by the presentation of a painting of the PGM's Coat of Arms, which still hang in the Norwich Masonic Hall.

The Provincial Grand Master who followed Hamon Le Strange was none other than the Rt Rev Bishop of Thetford and it is, in these days, rewarding to recall that at his installation he spoke these words:

> To be a Provincial Grand Master anywhere is a place even for a Bishop, but to be called to exercise that office in the Province of Norfolk is, I feel, an absolutely unique experience for a Bishop. In the ecclesiastical world Suffragan Bishops and Provinces are a long way apart but in the world of Masonry these things present no difficulties. . . . Brethren, it is spring time, everything is bursting with new life. Let that be the prophecy of our Province in every department of its work and all under the eye of the Great Architect of the Universe. That is the Spirit that will lead us to progress and victory.

Such are the words for Norwich that we would love to see re-echoed from such leaders in these days.

Opposite; Top: *The Bowers temple showing the Master's and Junior Warden's pedestals.*

Opposite; Bottom: *Two eighteenth century aprons.*

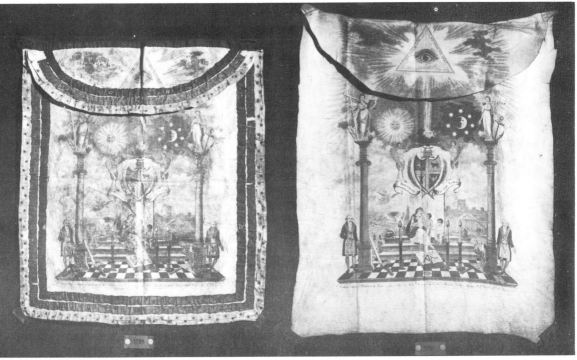

At the meeting of the Provincial Grand Lodge at Aylsham the committee produced its plans for the extensions and alterations at 47 Giles Street, and in appreciation of their labours the same body was made the Directorate of the Masonic Association there to carry the scheme into effect. A pledge of 1000 guineas from the Province was a first contribution towards the £13,100 estimated as the total cost involved. Before the project could be completed the Bishop of Thetford had died in his sleep and six masonic brethren carried his coffin at the funeral service in Norwich Cathedral.

It was in his memory that in 1929 the Pro Grand Master, Lord Ampthill, attended by yet another Bishop, of Colchester, as Grand Chaplain came to consecrate the new Temple and to dedicate the bronze portrait plaque of the Bishop made by Miss Maudie Buckingham. Six architects had entered the competition for the work and four had actually submitted plans. Though the work went to Stanley J. Wearing, the runner up had been Ernest J. Buckingham, both of them members of the craft. The results of their labours were to provide a New Temple to seat at least 200 brethren, with changing rooms and toilets; a second stage including a new supper room, kitchens and servery; and, finally, alterations and improvements to the present building and some refurnishing of it. In the final arrangements for this work to be carried out it had been decided that control of the company should in effect be in the hands of the Provincial Grand Lodge, and it is still the case that when one enters this building one senses that here is the heart of Norfolk freemasonry. It is also to be remembered that the laying of the foundation stone on 30 May, 1928, was also carried out in memory of the Bishop by no less a person than HRH the Prince of Wales (the later King Edward VIII). The miniature stone and tripod used by the Prince on that special day are now on view in the Provincial museum.

It was appropriate that the first Provincial meeting held by the next Bishop to be Provincial Grand Master of Norfolk, the Rt Rev Percy Mark Herbert, Bishop of Norwich, was held in the Bishop Bowers temple at St Giles Street. Sadly, on the day itself, the PGM was not well and had to write to the brethren instead. His closing sentence again set a seal on what he, as a very orthodox church leader, saw as the complementary nature of our Craft:

> May the Great Architect enable us all in our several ways to serve our Country through our Masonic Fellowship as builders of the Future on the foundation of obedience to the extreme of the Sacred Law.

If only for its association with these two fine episcopal exemplars of the Craft this hall would be memorable.

In 1945 Bp Herbert referred with approval to the decision made that day to name the present larger temple after Bishop Bowers and the smaller one 'Hamon le Strange'. He also thanked the Bowers and Union lodges for defraying the expense of placing the respective inscriptions over the entrance to these halls.

Thirty years later an arrangement was made between the Board of the Norwich Masonic Association Ltd and the Norwich Masonic Club for the latter to occupy both Nos 47 and the adjoining 49 St Giles Street. WBro E. H. Buckingham was this time the architect who arranged the present happy combination of the two properties so that by 1975 there was the completion of what we now see, on entering this Masonic Hall, as a most spacious and commodious entertainment area. It has enabled those gathering there to meet with a sense of style and it rightly gives to visitors a feeling of relaxation and ease before they have the delight of either sharing in the work in the temples or looking at the treasures of the library and museum.

It was in the carrying out of these alterations that necessary rearrangements were made to the latter which revealed in a new way the designs and workmanship of certain eighteenth and early nineteenth century jewels that had belonged to earlier stages of Norwich freemasonry. In the forefront of these are the jewels made by Meyer Levi, who subsequently took the name John Herbert. In *White's Norfolk* of 1836 he is mentioned as a 'herald chaser and hair worker, 31 Pottergate Street' and the marks of his workmanship here prove that this is the very same craftsman. His name also appears in the list of Angel Lodge No 112 which moved from Yarmouth where his father was a member (Samuel Levi, a 'slop', or old over-garments, seller, aged 46) to Norwich where Meyer is shown as having been initiated in 1822. In 1827 he is recorded as having been baptised, as a converted Jew, at St Stephen's church in the city, and his wife, Hannah, was baptised with him. They became Mr and Mrs John Herbert.

Some of the Meyer Levi Mark jewels.

His promotion in No 112 was rapid for he was Secretary in 1824, JW in 1825, SW from 1826-9 (*sic*) and WM in 1830, attending Provincial Grand Lodge in that capacity. Astonishingly it was in 1831 that the Provincial Grand Secretary and IPM of No 112 wrote to the Grand Secretary that in order to put a stop to 'the unmasonic and ungentlemanly feeling which existed among the members' they had decided to dissolve this lodge that was founded in 1751. One would like to hope that it had nothing to do with feeling against the Master's previous faith. He, at any rate, joined the Social lodge in April that year and was SW by October, Chaplain in November, reaching the chair again, via the Treasurer's and Warden's chairs, by January 1838.

The jewels he produced are not only charming but also distinctive and bore his mark of 'M.L.' or 'J.H.'. Before looking at these in some detail it is as well to recall that, as in other parts of the country, many Craft lodges by the early nineteenth century were involved in many more degrees than just those of the Craft. Hence, in the minute book of Union Lodge (then No 68) for 24 July, 1818, we read of the Royal Arch Chapter (Royal George) which was attached to it. On 23 January, 1820, the Deputy Provincial Grand Master proposed in a meeting of the same lodge: 'That all the expenses necessary for providing dresses and other preparations for the various degrees of Masonry such as Royal Arch, Knights Templar, Ark and Mark be borne by Lodge 68, that lodge taking the fees for conferring of any of the above degrees.' On the next Lodge night that same brother held a KT Conclave, at the same time, in an adjoining room!

It is in a 'Mark Register Book' dating from 1818 and belonging to the Union Lodge here, that we find the particulars of Meyer Levi's own advancement and his 'mark'—a 'Globe included in Compass and Square and inscribed in a serpent' (1824).

There were discovered in the Provincial library no less than seven prints of jewels with different emblems, which were evidently 'pulls' made by Meyer Levi's printers as a record from jewels he made. The jewel marked as No 5 (see illustration) shows almost exactly the same design as his personal mark. Of the others we know that the one showing a square and compasses extended and surrounding a circle with the Hebrew letters making 'shalom' (peace, perfection) was the mark of the Rev Samuel Titlow (Master of the Lodge of Eleusinian Mysteries) and the one with a cross belonged to John Lysaght Pennefather. What is more interesting is that four of the actual jewels fashioned by Meyer Levi are on view in the museum here and this one with the cross is amongst those displayed. What is a puzzle is why most of the jewels have 8 letters S K O I H T H W S whilst two of them, including the one belonging to Mr Titlow, have only 7! Moreover the letters used here are certainly not those now familiar to modern Mark Masters. To a student they were, in the Levi arrangement, much nearer to the Royal Arch arrangement, which would make sense as the degrees were previously conveyed.

Another delightful and intriguing jewel in this collection is that for the Royal Ark Mariner, with its olive-branch-bearing Dove pointing down on to an equilateral triangle, within which are still two more aligned triangles. The outer one has G.L.M. at its corners (Grand Lodge of Mariners or Grace, Love and Mercy) and the inner triangle has the initials of *N*oah, *S*hem and *J*apheth. At the heart of the inner triangle is a finely drawn ark on the waters with what looks like a cloud or ampersand above it. What is also interesting is that, like the Mark jewels already mentioned, this RAM item is suspended by a 'green' ribbon, and not one of the present many hues.

The next major item in this Hall is the 'Norfolk' or 'Flaming' sword which was presented by Bro William Rainger on becoming the first master of the new Lodge of Unanimity No 590 in Norwich. That was in December 1832. The blade is engraved on each side with many masonic emblems including the three figures of Faith, Hope and Charity. On the pillars of an arch near the hilt are 'L' on the left and '590' on the right, whilst the maker's name, 'S. Chambers, Birmingham, Sword Cutler to the Honble. Board of Ordnance' is also given. The scabbard is of brass, the grip of ivory with brass ornamental bands and a lion's head of brass at the end. The guard is of an entwined serpent on each side. It is similar in style to the Grand Lodge of the Antients' State Sword and it is noteworthy that both the Grand Lodge and the Lodge No 112 to which Rainger first belonged both started in 1751!

The wavy blade of a State Sword may, as Dr Hammond claimed, typify a 'Flame ascending to Heaven or, equally, the ascending of prayer.' As a lodge

Left: *A stone 'tracing board' (?) with distinctive masonic symbols.* Right: *A late eighteenth-century Ark Mariner jewel.*

sword it is more likely to be a form of other such swords in this series (see Alnwick)
and represent that flaming sword with which the angel kept Adam and Eve from
the Garden of Eden after their fall. It was thus ideally the form of a tyler's sword
for unwanted visitors. What is interesting here is that in this museum there are
other uses of much more strongly designed wavy swords in Meyer Levi's Past
Masters' jewels. Could it be that as he was a close colleague of Rainger he might
have influenced the latter in the kind of sword to give to his new lodge, when the
unpleasantness of No 112 had led to its closure?

We have already made mention of Perseverance Lodge and no visit to this Hall
would be complete without reference to the exquisite set of seals that belong to
those brethren from the turn of the eighteenth century. (See illustrations.) The first
is a simple one with the No 294, which number it held until 1814 (a gladius over a
square and compasses); the second is a much more decorative seal with No 374
which lasted until 1832 (two columns and globes with an altar on three steps
between and on it a VSL; above, an all-seeing eye with rays onto a square and

Examples of the seals that are on display at Norwich showing their excellent condition.

compasses with a G between, and around the columns the usual plumb, level, ladder, crossed wands, sun, moon and stars). The third is the Royal Arch chapter seal with 294 clearly changed to 374 (three concentric broken arches with an all-seeing eye darting its rays through the apertures to a G in space, above the VSL bearing a square and compasses). It almost certainly dates to 1799. The fourth seal is that of RAM lodge showing the number 258 (1832-63) and showing an ark sideways on, floating on the waters with a dove flying over the prow bringing an olive-leaf. On the edge of the matrix is the date 1802 so the numbers must also have been altered twice! The last seal is that of the Knights Templar degree and the number is 374 (it carries an equilateral triangle with a three-stepped Latin cross, five-pointed star, flaming sword, skull and crossbones within the triangle and 'Memento Mori' beneath it). The remarkable value of these seals is that not only are they in such perfect condition and showing what all lodges at the Union were meant to possess but they prove that whatever may have been said at the Union of the two Grand lodges these other degrees continued to be worked regularly.

One more item in the well-stocked and arranged museum must take our eye. It is a miniature tracing board or display piece of stone, intricately carved and serving as a perfect item for instruction in a Craft lodge. Its provenance seems to be Scotland for it has a fine thistle beneath the keystone-arch that surmounts the piece. It was probably first used in pre-Union days for at the centre of this item is the extended square and compasses with a G between but the position of these items is as for the FC degree. As an early form of the small board so often used in Emulation lodges to explain the Master's degree it is a truly fascinating relic. (See 'Taunton', vol 1, *Masonic Halls of England* (the South).)

NOTTINGHAM

The Masonic Hall in Goldsmith Street

WILLIAM, 6TH DUKE OF PORTLAND, was appointed to be the 7th Provincial Grand Master of the masonic Province of Nottinghamshire and was installed on 7 July, 1898. He was to rule for 35 years; as a man of great charm and with a very strong sense of responsibility his influence on the Province was both marked and memorable. He was a great landowner and a very prominent figure in public life, both locally and in London. The Nottinghamshire brethren of those days were exceedingly fortunate in their leader as many of them realised when he invited 900 brethren and their ladies to Welbeck in 1899.

In 1903 the Duke appointed as his Deputy the Rev Henry Telford Hayman and this has been described as 'the most notable event that ever occurred in Nottinghamshire Freemasonry'. Certainly the expansion of the Province under this combined leadership during the next 30 years was remarkable. The Duke regularly attended the Annual meetings of the Province and presided at innumerable stone-layings, of churches, schools and hospitals, whilst his Deputy visited the lodges and carried out the normal ceremonial work of the Province.

In 1905 the strength of the Province was 1005 but at a summer meeting in 1907 the attendance was 1900. When the Duke took over in 1898 the number of lodges under his rule was 18 and by the time he relinquished the post and allowed his faithful colleague, then *Canon* Hayman, to succeed him as Provincial Grand Master, the number of lodges had increased by another 32. The majority of these had started after the war of 1914-18 and not a few of them were meeting in Nottingham itself.

A first reference to the need for a larger Masonic Hall in Nottingham had been made at the December Annual Meeting in 1910. The General Purposes Committee had had the question under consideration and had appointed a sub-committee to go thoroughly into the matter and 'if possible, arrange some scheme in conjunction with the present Masonic Hall Company.... "When one considers," he continued "that Leicester and other Provinces have provided themselves with suitable buildings, I think that Nottingham should not lag behind ..."'

During the next two years little progress was to be made especially as one leaseholder in Belgrave Square was objecting to the erection of a masonic hall in that vicinity. This obstacle at last overcome an emergency meeting held in 1913 resolved to request 'the purchase of the freehold premises in Chaucer Street for a new Masonic Hall and buildings, obtain plans and do all that may be necessary for the attainment of that object... The area of the site was 2,660 sq.yards' and it was almost opposite the Midland Blind Institution, with a price of £2900! Alas, the project was at last under weigh when the advent of the War led to the view that it 'was deemed politic to defer this undertaking to more propitious times'.

With this unexpected and unnatural break of wartime it is an opportunity for the reader to look back briefly at the earliest years of the Province and see that there had been provision for masonry in this growing city and masonic centre. As early as 1847 the Provincial Grand Master stated his intention of always assembling the Provincial Grand Lodge at the Exchange Rooms on the 27th day of January, that being 'the birthday of the late lamented Grand Master, his Royal Highness the Duke of Sussex. . .'. For such meetings a 'proper Banner' was now required and the present Hall is proud to have it still displayed. In 1854, August, however, a special meeting of Prov. Grand Lodge was held at the George IVth Hotel though they were back at the Exchange Rooms and Flying Horse for the testimonial meeting and banquet to the first PGM (Col Wildman).

The next Provincial Grand Master died of a lingering disease at the age of 53 and was succeeded by his son, the 6th Duke of Newcastle. His installation was marked in a most unusual manner, as is revealed in the present Masonic Hall at Nottingham, by a poster preserved and framed in the museum there. The New Theatre was taken over by the freemasons for a 'Grand Masonic Night' with the proceeds given to the Charities of the town. The brethren are recorded as having appeared in 'FULL MASONIC COSTUME' (*sic*) and the programme apparently consisted of Planche's brilliant Comedietta in two acts, 'Court Favour!' and the Opening of the Magnificent Pantomime, 'The House that Jack Built'. It was certainly a novel way of celebrating the beginning of a new reign.

At the next Provincial Grand Lodge meeting a resolution was passed that 'in the opinion of this Lodge it is desirable that a Masonic Hall should be secured for the Province' and hence the machinery to secure this end was established. Three years later some progress was reported, for in March 1879 the committee revealed that a convenient site in Goldsmith Street had been purchased and plans drawn up for the erection of a suitable property at a total cost, including furniture *and* decoration, of £6000. Three more years later the Provincial Grand Lodge was actually held there on 30 November, 1882, with a Grand Masonic Ball to follow. The local newspaper was moved to surprising eloquence:

> The strikingly gorgeous regalia of the Craft, mingling with the fair forms of the ladies, the gay throng being studded here and there with a military uniform or the naval blue, together make a combination which no other gathering can approach in point of effect. . . . The spacious salon of the Albert Hall had been transformed into a vast fairy-like palace. In the work of decoration the Lodge banners and other insignia of the Craft played a conspicuous part. . . .

Is it conceivable that the reporter was himself one of the brethren?

The premises in Goldsmith Street were clearly limited in scope. At the annual meeting on 5 December, 1889, only 55 brethren could join in the banquet there, whilst in 1894 it was reported that the heavy expenses incurred for the repair of the organ meant that no grants could be made to the main masonic Charities as had hitherto been the case. On the other hand there was a determined effort to establish a base for the increasing number of treasured items that are nowadays on view at Goldsmith Street, for in December 1895 the Prov. Grand Secretary reported the setting up of the masonic library and museum. Those present then would have been delighted had they been able to look forward and see the results of this initiative. One of the first items to be added to the collection was the silver-mounted mallet used by the Duke of Portland in laying the foundation stone of the Gordon Boys' New Home in Cranmer Street, which is now the Nottinghamshire Teachers' Centre.

By 1905 the members attending the Provincial Grand Lodge were already too large to be accommodated at the Goldsmith Street hall and hence they moved again to the Albert Hall—the scene of the colourful Ball. It was not the most satisfactory venue in the December weather and the Deputy Prov GM (the Revd H. T. Hayman) is recorded as saying that they were 'An audience of two hundred, exiles from the blessings of ventilation, all simmering together in their own animal heat'. It was no doubt similar experiences that led to the proposal for a larger hall in Nottingham—the one that foundered only with the advent of hostilities in 1914.

It was thus at an Emergency Meeting of the Province in October 1919 that the matter was reopened. The 1913 scheme was now thought to be too expensive and 'the site, with its houses which had sheltered Belgian refugees all through the War, was considered not sufficiently central'. It was therefore decided to accept the offer made by the Nottingham Blind Institution for the land which had been acquired and to begin fresh negotiations for extending and enlarging the existing Hall in Goldsmith Street. A year later the PGM referred to the urgent need to raise £4,000 to complete the purchase of the properties adjoining the previous masonic hall so that the extensions could be begun, and within another 12 months the local masons had provided threequarters of the sum. By 1923 the Provincial Grand Lodge was able to purchase all the shares in the existing Masonic Hall Company to form a new one.

It was in this same year that the Duke of Portland completed 25 years of service to Nottinghamshire masonry and the portrait which was contributed to by every brother in the Province to mark the event still proudly hangs in the Ionic temple of the present Hall. The Duke's happy announcement in 1924 was that, as it had been found impossible to extend the existing Hall satisfactorily, it had been decided to construct an entirely new one on the Goldsmith Street site. The cost of this venture was going to be £60,000 and it was made clear that they could only proceed with the work when some third of that amount had been subscribed. Another future portrait for the Hall was however produced when Canon Hayman, the Deputy PGGM, was presented with his likeness executed by the same Royal Academician as the one that had painted the Duke.

Considering that brethren were being asked to give to the central Masonic Million Fund for the erection of the Great Queen Street building in London at the same time it is a great tribute to the masons here that within two years of the original appeal for Goldsmith Street £17,250 had been provided. As if to mark this stage of the work a new banner was produced to replace the one that had first appeared in 1850, though, interestingly, there is no mention whatsoever of it being dedicated.

In December 1928 the Annual Meeting took place at the Albert Hall Institute for the first duty to be undertaken was to proceed in procession to Goldsmith Street where the PGM laid the foundation stone of the present structure. The ceremony was fully reported in the local press as 'picturesque and impressive' and

The Ionic temple entrance.

the minute book is enlivened with photographs of the occasion, together with an artist's impression of how the new hall would look—at least until 1971. The architect, WBro C. E. Howitt, presented a gold trowel to the Duke and WBro G. E. Butcher offered an ivory maul. Both of these items are also carefully preserved in the cases of the museum. The PGM contrasted the £20,000 raised so far by 46 lodges with the effort needed by 7 lodges meeting in Nottingham in 1881 to find £6,000 for the previous hall on this site.

By 1930 the Duke was able to report that 'every bit of the new furniture for the Masonic Hall had been obtained at actual manufacturers' cost price so that the new building, due to be dedicated by the Grand Secretary, VWor Bro Sir Percy Colville-Smith, in 1931, could be economically as well as suitably fitted out. A contemporary brochure described the finished Hall as 'an important addition to Nottingham's public buildings' and anyone observing it today will have to agree.

In the museum display the visitor will find a most lovely case, inlaid with mother of pearl, in which were handed over all the trowels and other mementoes that had been presented to the Duke of Portland during his very popular and fruitful reign. It is a most gracious and fitting token of the affection with which this PGM was viewed by his brethren and his post and the emblems on that case—the all-seeing eye radiating upon an ark bearing the VSL and standing between two lights with a winged hour-glass on one side and the tasselled cushion on the other only reflects the sacred, intensely human, illuminating and dedicated way in which this reign as a ruler in the Craft was begun, continued and ended.

Sadly, some of the items that should have graced the present museum and rooms of the Goldsmith Street Hall were destroyed when, just after midnight on 9 May 1941, the enemy dropped a bomb in the middle of the Masonic Hall "completely destroying the Doric Temple, the dining room and its suite, and doing severe damage to the ante-room and Corinthian Temple, the corridor, main staircase and ante-chamber to the Ionic Temple'. Surprisingly, a bust of Canon Hayman, the newly-unveiled picture of WBro Starling and most of the effects in the heart of the museum were unaffected though there was a noticeable bulge in the front wall on the street side. The very heavy doors at the entrance finished up across the road but the records of the Province in the Secretary's office were unharmed as also were the banners and other lodge regalia in the basement. It was a serious blow, but as those attending the installation of the Royal Ark Mariners six days after the blitz showed, it was not such a disaster that freemasonry could not continue.

Today the scars of war no longer show. 45 years of further and continuous use have mellowed the signs of repair and given to the wide and impressive frontage almost the sense of having been there from time immemorial. Only the modern style of the huge, towering pillars that flank the porticoed entrance, the double-glazed frame windows and the well-used car park at the side make clear that this was a new hall built for a modern age of freemasonry. When in 1965 WBro. C. H. V. Elliott was installed as the next Provincial Grand Master they were able to sit 206 brethren down in the Ionic Dining Room and another 106 in the Corinthian, but by 1971, when still further extensions were possible by the purchase of all the remaining houses in Belgrave Square nearby even the Provincial Grand Lodge meeting could take place in the magnificent Belgrave Suite.

It is time, however, to look at last inside this fine addition to Nottinghamshire masonry and to rejoice over what has been an achievement that will ever be remembered. As with many large and important buildings such as this, the basement is mainly given over to storage. Part of it, however, is set aside to provide amenities for the Nottinghamshire Masonic Club, which is open to membership by any freemason on application. Here are to be found a bar, television lounge, billiard and card rooms. On the ground floor there is also a very well appointed and comfortable lounge bar of more generous proportions, and here the members can have morning coffee and afternoon teas. Lunches are also provided in the nearby dining room.

The Corinthian Dining Room is in constant daily—or rather evening—use and it is of dignified and elegant proportions. The nearby kitchens are staffed by one head chef, four cooks and six other helpers. Across the foyer from the Goldsmith Street entrance is the Ionic Dining Room, and its own ante-room, that in turn gives access to the offices of the Provincial Grand Master, Grand Secretary and their attendant staff. The ante-room has a war memorial tablet and a sculptured portrait of the Rev. Canon Hayman.

The dining room here is the largest in this part of the present building and has a distinct sense of superiority, in its elegance of decoration, over the one across the hall. It has witnessed many splendid and glittering occasions and was, before the opening of the latest Belgrave Suite, the location for many Ladies' Festivals. It is here that the last Provincial Grand Master was to entertain the many principal guests at the Province's Bi-centenary celebrations.

Returning to the foyer we may now mount the most ample staircase, on which a plaque commemorating the bi-centenary has now been placed. This was given by the Newark ladies and it takes its honoured place alongside a photograph-portrait of the present Grand Master. The staircase leads onto a most handsome landing and immediately before the visitor are two very distinctive old lodge chairs, rightly roped to prevent anyone from damaging them.

The one on the right of the small alcove is a Master's chair belonging to the Royal Sussex Lodge No 402. It was presented by the first Master, Col Thomas Wildman who was also Provincial Grand Master from 1823 to 1826. The chair is a perfect example of the Chippendale style of around 1750. Above the chair and on the alcove wall is the patent of the Colonel as PGM. His jewel is found in the nearby museum.

The other chair is thought to be one of a pair of Wardens' chairs for the same lodge and is certainly mentioned in the Royal Sussex inventories of the early nineteenth century. The chair comes from the period when the lodge met in the Assembly Rooms, George IV Hotel, the Exchange Rooms and Guildhall before being in the old Masonic Hall here. Beside this and the chair referred to above there are also two ancient globes set on tripods which are specially notable as having the Zodiac engraved on the rim that surrounds each of the spheres. The

Left: *An early apron.* Centre: *A Chippendale Master's chair c1750.*
Right: *One of the ancient globes.*

picture on the alcove wall showing the underground temple at Welbeck Abbey is also worth noting.

Off the landing to the right and up some stairs is the smallest of the upstairs temples, the Doric, and its contemporary style of decoration contrasts clearly with those that we are yet to see. In actual fact, this is rather the Tuscan *suite*, for in addition to the comfortable, if modest, room for ceremonies there are also robing arrangements, committee room, bar and dining facilities. The temple, like all the others, has an organ, though in keeping with its more modern origin the organ here is an electronic one.

Outside the Doric suite and in the corridor there are some beautifully arranged old documents which include an 1814 Guernsey KT certificate, belonging to the No 45 Lodge of Friendship in the 4th Garrison Battalion; an 1860 KT certificate issued by Abbey Chapter of the Nottinghamshire Encampment; a Kadosh certificate used in the KT Encampment of 1850; a Royal Arch clearance certificate of the Humber Chapter No 65 of 6 October, 1835; a lodge certificate of 1775 with signatures of T over H issued to a Bro Elliot, and a Percy Lodge certificate from Morpeth, dated 1813. The collection here, apart from what is found elsewhere, would honour any hall.

The nearby Corinthian temple is a sharp contrast to the Doric as it is more reflective of the style which was relevant to the late twenties. It has a pipe organ. Outside the Corinthian suite we notice the patent of Col Wilman as Grand Superintendent in 1825, whilst alongside this frame is an unusual set of regalia—a Grand Bible Bearer's collar in the Scottish Constitution showing a jewel with the open VSL surrounded by abundant foliage.

Passing back along the landing one notes at the stair-head a large display of masonic jewels and before we enter the Ionic temple with its five steps and two large marble pillars outside the entrance (giving quite the impression of a minor Solomon's Temple) one has reached that area of the first floor where glass cases contain pottery, glassware and many other masonic items of special interest—both local and more general—to which in part some mention has already been paid.

Of particular importance, but only as samples of a very considerable collection, one mentions a large stoneware hot water bottle in the shape of a setting maul and bearing many masonic emblems; an 1805 'frog in the mug' piece which may well have surprised many a brother 'in his cups'; a set of Bohemian red firing glasses, a seventeenth-century dark-green glass Bristol bottle with masonic emblems etched on it, including the Sun, Moon and stars, an ashlar, ladder, coffin, level, plump and rule. There are also three very well preserved 'verge' watches with their emblem-decorated faces, from 1804, 1811 and 1817, and a charmingly inlaid knife box of masonic provenance, dated 1780. A great feast for a masonic visitor.

The Ionic temple is in fact the largest and most impressive of the ceremonial rooms. It is the main portrait 'gallery' of the whole Hall and some of its major figures there have already been detailed. The organ console is particularly fine and the decoration is especially rich.

Across the ante-room, with its special exhibits, is the private room of the Provincial Grand Master and alongside that is the library, which has the theatre bills, manuscripts, and documents as well as old regalia, jewels and, of course, some very valuable books.

The Kirkwall scroll, the marvellous copy of the Old Charges, and the Newstead

Lodge documents including a demit certificate of 1814, a summons of 1806 and lodge certificates of 1805 and 1820, both sealed, and the warrant of 1775 all merit close attention. A Royal Arch certificate of 1788 with words from St John, chapter 1, and mentioning the passing of the chair is also of peculiar interest these days whilst a Royal Ark Apron with rainbow edges, a fine design of the ark, sea, rainbow and dove on the front and a lettered triangle on the flap, adds to the uniqueness of this local collection. The KT student will also have a great deal to note here as well as upstairs.

To show how the present hall has continued to serve and be of real worth to the masons of Nottingham we shall need to retrace our steps along the landing and descend to the impressive new Belgrave suite that now occupies the rear of the premises. It has enabled parties of 250 masons and their ladies to be entertained comfortably and it is, not surprisingly, a popular place for private and special functions. It is of particular value in serving a growing and flourishing Province and it has continued to be as useful up the present as it was on the bi-centenary occasion of 1983.

As any mason leaves this building, and not least as he pauses on his way to consider once more the façade in Goldsmith Street, he may well reflect that here is a place that has its own store of memories of days past, and a sure means of encouraging memories for all who see it and use it today.

Masonic Hall Goldsmith Street.

*The Ancients pedestal and
Cathedral panel at Peterborough.*

PETERBOROUGH

The Masonic Hall in a Cathedral City

PETERBOROUGH IS DESCRIBED in the third edition of the Everyman Encyclopaedia (1950) as being 'a well-built city, containing many fine buildings and kept remarkably neat'. Since then there has been much development as a 'New Town' with a varied mix of offices and industry and there is a main-line junction though without the previous large workshops for the manufacture of railway stock. There are also facilities for the manufacture of bricks. This reference to a city that had grown and prospered considerably since the end of the last war is no less appropriate for our present purpose for it is only fitting that in a place that has always been a local brick-making centre we should be visiting a Masonic Hall that has incorporated a good deal of brick into its structure.

You will find the Hall as you approach the city centre from the north, though you might be forgiven for passing by its anonymous street exterior, with its framed windows below and mullioned ones above. The entrance door is also inconspicuous in North Street, round the corner of the building, though the curious may notice in the wall above it a niche which shows the crossed keys of St Peter, the arms of the diocese, adopted by the oldest lodge within. The exterior, however, is by no means an adequate indication of the fascinating history and contents that can be discovered inside. It is to that history that we ought first to turn.

In his record of the Provincial Grand Lodge of Northamptonshire and Huntingdonshire, written in 1912, WBro Thomas Dorman begins by referring to the Right Honourable George Fermor, Earl of Pomfret, Lord Lempster, as the first Provincial Grand Master, and his name appears in the dedication of a sermon preached at St John's Church, Peterborough, on 26 July, 1802, when the preacher was the Rev Samuel Oliver, father of the more famous Dr Oliver. It was to mark the occasion of the inauguration of the lodge of St Peter No 596 which subsequently met at the Angel Hotel in Narrow Street.

Though this, the first recorded lodge in Peterborough, bore the same name as the St Peter's Lodge No 442, that has its home in the present Hall, it should be noted that it was not strictly the same warranted unit. The first St Peter's started as lodge No 160B under the Grand Lodge of the 'Antients' or 'Athol' tradition and its strange number was because it employed a warrant transferred from a lodge that first met at the 'Queen of Hungary's Head, Norwich'. What then seems to have happened was that this lodge left the Athol Grand Lodge within the year and by Christmas was being constituted afresh under the premier Grand Lodge in which it took the number 596.

Its importance locally and in connection with the present building is that it was in this first St Peter's Lodge that the renowned Dr Oliver, the voluminous commentator on, and historian of, masonic matters, was initiated and we shall be looking later at what is generally considered to be the pedestal at which this took place. Into this lodge there came also, as a joining member, that Dr Crucefix, whose concern for the poor and 'decayed' masons of his day led to his campaign on behalf of the institution now called the RMBI.

This lodge lasted only 26 years, however, and was then erased, along with 58 others, for want of communication with London. The lodge ceased to meet, and an 'incomer', a Scot called Thomas Ewart (later to be Deputy PGM) found its papers and revived it. On finding that it had been erased he and seven other masons then applied in 1836 for a new warrant that they might meet every first Thursday at the Windmill Inn and under the title of the Crucefix Lodge. An extract from the Freemasons' Quarterly Review of the time explains what happened next.

> Peterborough, Jan. 14th. The brethren in this city were convened by special summons to assemble on this day, at the Masonic Hall, contiguous to the Windmill Inn, to receive Dr Crucefix, the J.D.C. of England, who had been directed by HRH the Duke of Sussex, M.W. Grand Master to constitute them as a lodge . . . The members are most anxious to evince their sense of obligation to Dr Crucefix, by having the Lodge named after him; for which compliment, however, there was not only no precedent, but it might have been productive of inconvenience; it was therefore, at the suggestion of the Grand Master, named the St. Peter's Lodge, and the blank was filled up by the Constitutor in open lodge.

The warrant now in the Lodge Room is a replacement of the original now sadly lost in a fire.

Whilst this was doubtless the right course at that time it is, I am sure, a matter for delight to know that these honoured brethren, one a constitutor and the other a member of St Peter's Lodge, are today recognised, by the attendance at the present Hall, of not only a Dr Oliver lodge and chapter, but also a Dr Crucefix Rose Croix chapter. The names of eminence have thus been linked with a place that will for ever be the richer for their service. Indeed, it is a good note that at a meeting of the Provincial Grand Lodge under the banner of St Peter's, in May 1843, "Graces, before and after the banquet, were pronounced by Dr Oliver" and 'Dr Crucefix was entrusted with the honour of proposing the health of the noble chairman, the Earl of Aboyne'. The occasion was especially touching because it was at a later stage of these proceedings that Dr Oliver replied to his toast as Deputy Provincial Grand Master by saying, 'I have arrived at the time of life when I ought to retire from the active business of Masonry; and as I began my Masonic careeer in St Peter's Lodge, it is highly probable that I shall close it in the same place by my appearance amongst you today'. Dr Oliver's Grand Lodge certificate is in the lodge room and his portrait (preserved by a descendant) is on the landing wall at the top of the new extension stairs.

In 1850 the brethren sat down to 'a most elegant banquet, prepared by Bro Biney, the worthy host of the Crown Hotel, which was characterised not only by every requisite, but by every dainty the season could afford'. Despite such evenings

The Senior Warden's pedestal with organ pipes behind.

the lodge members were anxious by 1859 to establish a more permanent centre for their work and possessions. A building committee was appointed and though, by March 1861, it was reported that 'until the lodge became better prepared to carry out Plans for a masonic hall it was advisable to remain in its present situation' the impetus had begun. By 30 December, 1862, there was news of a 'building in view, at a price calculated to meet with the approval of the lodge'.

The site was the one we see today in Lincoln Road and it was the property of Mr R. S. Tomlin. With moderate alterations it was considered adequate for the purposes of the lodge, even with allowing that the lower floor be let to Messrs Elgood, Brewers, of Wisbech at a rental of £20 per annum. It is surely appropriate that even to this day that floor is the one that continues to provide refreshment— albeit not only of beer and ale—for the brethren. The building was secured by a deposit of £100 from the Lodge funds and by 2 April, 1863, Bro F. G. Buckle, the Provincial Grand Secretary and Committee Chairman, reported the final purchase of the property at £350. At the same time the lodge's number changed to its present 442.

The lodge now set about making the new 'home' into fully workable premises. They first built a wooden partition about six feet away from the south end wall (the present 'East end' of the temple upstairs) and this provided a storeroom which was to serve until 1939. At the opposite end they constructed a similar partition some 8 feet from the existing wall and this allowed an area of only 8 feet square for the Provincial Officers to robe and for the Tyler then to use as a preparation room. In addition the partition was pierced at the top of the stairs by a door for entry into the lodge, but, in order to create a greater sense of privacy, another member of the Buckle family presented the lodge with a large oak screen that projected into the lodge another 3 ft 6 in and against which the S Warden's chair was placed. There were also curtains between the ends of the screen and the partition so that those entering had to part one or either of these 'veils' before seeing the arrangements of the temple itself. It meant that the lodge room itself was cosy but comparatively restricted and was certainly not such as to give the sense of space and dignity that pervades today.

The room was dedicated as the Masonic Hall, Peterborough on 4 November 1864 by the new Provincial Grand Master, the Duke of Manchester. He had opened the Special Provincial Grand Lodge previously in the Wentworth Hotel and then the whole assembly marched in procession, fully clothed and preceded by an escort of His Grace the Duke's own mounted troops! That must certainly have drawn the attention of the 'uninstructed and popular world' to this building then even if they now probably know little of it.

Some forty years later it had become clear that with the growth of both the lodge and the Craft locally it was proper to consider the use of the whole of the premises. It was decided not to re-let the ground floor but to adapt it for dining purposes. Some local builders, Lucas, were commissioned to make the necessary alterations. Partitions were erected in the same places as the ones on the floor above, so that at the far end of the intervening dining area there was a kitchen and crockery store, whilst at the near end there was an entry hall for cloaks and a shut-off bar and Steward's room under the Tyler's room upstairs.

The odd feature of the Hall at that time is shown by the outline, clearly seen on the brick face in North Street, of what was the only entry point to the hall. This was a flight of six stone steps up to a substantial platform that reached out into the street as well as into the building. It was, of course, the original loading bay for the horse-drawn drays that came to collect the barrels of beer that were once stored in the lower part of the building. The platform just met the level of the floor of the carts that lined up outside. For the brethren it meant six cold steps up to enter the door, and six more down to the hall inside. There are still those who can remember the hazardous task of helping some old Past Master who had dined too well and not too wisely down the frozen steps into the street! It is not surprising that the lodge at last agreed to light the steps with electric light in 1903.

The single chimney protruding from the roof on the side street of the present Hall serves to remind its occupants of the large fireplaces that once were the only means of heating both the temple and dining area. The red-bricked chimney breast upstairs has now been covered over and thus deprived the visitor of what must have been an especial feature of unusual design. (For those who are interested in masonic hall fireplaces see the ones at Cheltenham and Poole). In 1925 the present heating and ventilation system was installed.

By 1939 the present and much more commodious temple and dining room

The secretary and treasurer's desk.

began to appear. The purchase of some neighbouring space in North Street and a legacy left by WBro Adams at the centenary in 1936, meant that the partitions in both areas could be dismantled. A new entrance hall with a suitable staircase was created and the upstairs area was enlarged to allow for more robing space and also a gracious museum and library room. What strikes one about the latter facilities is the care and attention given to the housing and arrangement of not only frames of masonic jewels or clothing from an earlier age, but also the records and books, including some of Dr Oliver's works.

It is, as one might expect, however, in the temple here that one is particularly aware of the age and dignity of this memorable hall. The new dimensions made possible in the last 50 years have mellowed with time and care and the whole seems as if it had been established from the outset in the mid-Victorian period. Though the room is not unduly lofty it is given a special sense of space by the plain and shallow curved ceiling with its gentle, seasoned golden texture. Originally it was a blue expanse with the usual stars. The east end, with its dark blue panels between the curved end of the roof and the cornice, is then contrasted by the rich brown Victorian stye wallpaper that runs across the whole area below carrying on it the 8 warrants or charters of the various lodges and chapters that meet here. In a time when the removal of such framed possessions is increasingly the mode elsewhere it is this that gives one the real sense of moving backwards in time and sensing that early Victorian age when Dr Oliver himself knelt to be obligated, in Peterborough, if not exactly here.

The lovely pedestal, well used but richly decorated on three sides, that stands before the Master is surely the one that Dr Oliver must himself have known. It carries on the front a large-sized representation of the arms of the Athol or Antients Grand Lodge—a shield bearing the four quarters of a rampant lion, an ambling ox, a man with his arms raised like Moses and an eagle with wings extended, with the ark of the convenant on its poles above and this covered with two of the wings of the cherubim that support the shield, they having three other wings attached to them. Above the wings is the cloudy canopy or shekinah with an effulgence of light in which are inscribed the Hebrew letters denoting the Deity,

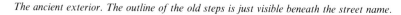

The ancient exterior. The outline of the old steps is just visible beneath the street name.

whilst at the foot of the panel and embracing the hoofed feet of the angels is a scroll carrying the words, 'Holiness to the Lord'. On the left of the pedestal facing it is a lady in late eighteenth century dress holding an anchor whilst on the right is another such lady with children. They, of course, represent Hope and Charity, whilst on the rear panel is a lady with a cross representing Faith. It is not at all surprising that the brethren of St Peter's Lodge hold this item of furniture in high regard and feel proud to have been able to preserve it through nearly two centuries.

Upon the top of the pedestal lies a crimson cushion with gold edging and four golden tassels and, at least in the case of St Peter's Lodge, a seventeenth-century version of the VSL. It is very well thumbed. There also stands one of the three candlesticks in the lodge, each of them fluted and then capped by the decoration due to the officer whose pedestal they adorn.

Yet this pedestal does not stand alone. It is part of a rich amalgam of items that focus the visitor's attention on the east end of the temple. Behind the pedestal is a square-stepped dais with three treads all covered in chequered pavement carpeting. The same decoration covers the two steps at the SW and the one step at the Junior Warden's place. On the top of the dais stands a light oak armchair, with royal red upholstery, lion-headed armrests, a richly carved backpiece including foliage and spiralled pillars and a circular headpiece in which stands a figure of St Peter. This chair is all the more impressive because it stands against a huge Cathedral chancel-, and Gothic-type, panel with tall triangular centrepiece and soaring finials that reach almost to the roof. It is exquisitely carved in rich, dark oak and carries three coats of arms, the badges of the oldest lodges on shields, and the following inscription:

This canopy was removed from Peterborough Cathedral when the choir east of the tower was dismantled in 1883 and was erected here with the two great pillars to commemorate the Bicentenary of the foundation of the Grand Lodge of England.

JUNE 1717	JUNE1917
W.Bro. John W. Crawley	W.M. No. 442
W.Bro. John E. Pointon	W.M. No. 2533
W.Bro Joseph Lazenby	W.M. No. 2596

This imposing feature and the chairs represent the ever close association which Peterborough masons have had with the Cathedral and its staff here. In 1870 we read of how close this link was.

The brethren, under the command of the Provincial GD of Ceremonies, were arranged under their respective banners in procession, and, preceded by the band of the 6th Peterborough Volunteer Rifle Corps, started from the lodge room at the Grand Northern Hotel at a quarter before two o'clock arriving at the Cathedral at 2. The streets were lined the whole distance with spectators. The Sermon was preached by the Rt. Rev. the Lord Bishop of the Diocese, Bro. William Connor Magee, D.D., D.C.L., to a vast congregation. The Cathedral being crowded with 5000 or 6000 persons, many of whom were seated nearly an hour before the service commenced. The Bishop made a pertinent appeal to his hearers on behalf of the funds for the Royal Masonic Boys' School and the Peterborough Dispensary. The kind and felicitious aid rendered by the Cathedral authorities elicited and merited the warmest approbation...

The same welcome was there in 1876 whilst in 1884 we have 800 masons attending on the Earl of Carnarvon, the Pro-Grand Master, as he came to lay the foundation stone of the new tower of the Cathedral. The Dean was to ask the Earl to lay the stone in full masonic form, whilst later it was the Bishop of Peterborough that was to propose the Earl's health. It is a setting for the return of which we ought devoutly to long and in this masonic hall we have a singular and lasting token of that mutual regard.

Again, the visitor will notice beside these ecclesiastical gifts two enormous pillars surmounted by the terrestrial and celestial globes. They reach to the panels above the cornice and they are adorned at the top with capitals, pomegranate seeds and lilywork. Being dark in colour they match the cathedral panel admirably and still further enhance the great east end centrepiece. That on the right facing east is J and is so marked, with B on the left. On the pillars appear this inscription:

> Two great pillars were erected
> by the Freemasons of Peterborough to
> commemorate the Bi-centenary of the
> foundation of the Grand Lodge of Engand.
>   JUNE 1717   JUNE 1917

Three delicate chandeliers illumine the room which is otherwise lit by concealed lighting. A vast chequered carpet with wide indented border and Chapter symbols covers the whole area of the floor and sets off the pale blue colour of the walls on which are placed fine oak frames holding the details of lodge masters and chapter principals.

At the west end of the room and behind the SW's chair is the casing of a pipe organ which complements the ecclesiastical furniture at the other end. Surmounting the pipes are four turrets with a triangular piece between. Above, on the blue area below the curved ceiling line is another decoration—a gold triangle surrounded by rays, with a bible open within it and on the bible the words, 'And God said, let there be light and there was light'. At the foot of the triangle is a plain cross and around that a flowing scroll with the well-known phrase—Brotherly Love, Relief and Truth. A level and a plumb on the left hand side of the centrepiece and a maul and chisel on the right complete this decoration. What is also interesting is that a touch of the past remains at the door where a curtain can be drawn over the entrance and thus restore the fashion of entry that earlier masons knew when the room was smaller.

Before we leave this temple we must pay attention to two further items of furniture that make this room the more distinctive. They are placed on the north side of the lodge and consist of a desk with a clock above it. The desk is reputed as having belonged, like the Master's pedestal, to the first St Peter's Lodge and this can be well believed for instead of being a desk behind which the Secretary and Treasurer sit it consists of two desks resting on one pedestal and facing each other with the people using them sitting with their backs at right angles to the wall. The benefit of such an arrangement in a room that was not too large, such as in a hotel or tavern, is obvious and it would have been no less useful in the earlier and more constricted room here. On the centre of the desk is a common inkwell whilst at the front of the desk, at its widest part, is a drawer. Against the wall the desk supports a charming pair of hooded lamps with curved silver brackets held together by a silver stem.

Above this desk and provided later, no doubt to complement the desk, is a fine Victorian clock. It has a curved triangular base, a centre panel on which are the name and no. of St Peter's and a square and compasses with the letter G between. The circular, white faced clock above is regularly in use and was ideal for marking those moments that secretaries have to record. It is, also, appropriately opposite the Junior Warden who might occasionally declare it 'High Time'.

It is not possible to include here all the treasures of this memorable place but as one passes again along the new landing it is good to see the well-preserved banner of the previous St Peter's Lodge with its No 596. Above a green scroll carrying the lodge name and place of Peterborough and between a square and compasses and level in gold at the top corners, one sees a red-based shield with two huge keys quartered by four pattée crosses, all in gold. This clear token of the Saint, set in a distinctive Christian context that would have pleased Dr Oliver so much, is then embraced by two huge clusters of oak leaves which emerge from some evergeen leaves of gold at the top of the shield. They have, rearing from them, what look like serpents, those emblems of wisdom and eternity. Yet at the centre of the top is a huge golden shell, reared vertically and exposing its grained interior. Its reminder of saintly pilgrimage is once more a fitting completion to the badge of this pre-Union assemblage. It is also a timely invitation to other masonic travellers to come and see this memorable hall and the well-established masonic connections that it so honourably preserves.

The old St Peter's Lodge banner.

SHREWSBURY

The Hall where all seats are for Freemasons

TWO HUNDRED YEARS ago, as the happily extant first minute books can tell us, there was founded in this county town of Shrewsbury a lodge bearing the appropriate name of 'Salopian'. The warrant of this lodge is dated 13 May 1788 and it constituted certain local brethren, including William Neale, the first Master, into a regular lodge with the No 1 (*sic*), 'to be opened at a House known by the sign of the Fox'. The Rev Francis Egerton was then Provincial Grand Master for Shropshire, and Major Charles Shirreff was his Deputy, and it was the latter who procured this chart for Salopian. It is today the oldest lodge in the Province. What is of special interest, as can be seen from observing the warrant kept in today's Masonic Hall, is that it was issued by the Province and not by Grand Lodge. All that we know further about the founders is that Bro William Cotton, the first Junior Warden, was landlord of the Trumpet Inn, and Bro John Beck was a banker and wine merchant. It is also worth noting that one of the first joining members was the then newly appointed County Surveyor of Shropshire, Thomas Telford, who had met Bro Hazeldine, an ironmaster.

The registered number of this lodge in the Moderns Grand Lodge register was actually 525, and the Fox Inn, where it was to meet for the first two years, was on a site which was later to be that of the Working Men's Hall. It had a fine courtyard in front of it but there was no frontage onto the neighbouring Princess Street or College Hill. Unconstitutionally the landlord, Mr James Trehearn, was initiated in the first year and was also made a member.

The lodge was soon hard at work and in the first six months there were 22 meetings, of which nine were called 'Lodges of Emergence'. 39 ceremonies were also performed. The work was recognised as rapid, for three brethren passed on 11 November 1788, were raised a week later. One dispensation was certainly given for the initiation of the Rev George Holland on the same night as he was ballotted for but as the 'Deputy Provincial Grand' was the brother who conducted the degree such a variation of the bye-laws was never questioned.

There were interchanges with the 'Barry Lodge', meeting at the Trumpet, and with the Lodge of Industry which belonged to Bridgnorth—especially on the Festival of St John. In 1800, and for the next ten years, the brethren were faced with the poll tax which was levied throughout the Craft to meet the expense of paying for the Freemasons' Hall in London. Lodges not meeting this charge were to be erased and it appears that two Shropshire lodges were struck off the Grand Lodge roll accordingly. A minute of 5 August 1800 shows the first dissatisfaction of the lodge with their own local accommodation at the Fox, when it was ordered 'that the ill-treatment of the lodge by Bro Trehearn should be inquired into'. In October notice was given of the intention to move to other quarters. Not surprisingly the move was to be to the Trumpet Inn which was situated in Hill's Lane, Mardol, but sadly it was not a successful venture.

In 1825, Bro Sir Andrew Vincent Corbet was Worshipful Master and seems to have made a vigorous effort to get a separate Masonic Hall built. On 31 January, when the matter was discussed in lodge, the sum of £320 was then and there subscribed by the brethren in £10 shares. The Worshipful Master offered to supply stone from his personal quarry at Grinshill, and even the Provincial Grand Master approved of the scheme and offered his assistance. Plans were ordered to be prepared, and success in quite a short time seemed likely, but the word getting around that the Salopian lodge members would be wholly responsible for all expenses involved the brethren insisted that the venture be a wholly private transaction—and that effectively killed the project! In the official history of the Shropshire Province written at the end of the nineteenth century there appears these relevant words:

> Other subsequent efforts to secure such a building in Shrewsbury had proved abortive, and its absence, sometimes greatly felt, is a standing disgrace to the Masons of the town . . .

In 1840 the Salopian brethren, who had moved to the Lion Hotel, were again dissatisfied and went to a room situated on the premises at the rear of the spot on which was erected subsequently the new Fire Headquarters and yet, though they fitted up this and a room below at considerable expense, they were to stay but three

St Michael's church now converted into a modern masonic hall.

years there. In 1843 the lodge, despite it having let off one of the rooms to the local Glee Club to raise capital, was driven away by lack of resources, closed its High Street 'home' and returned to another previous tenancy at the Raven and Bell Inn.

Meanwhile, a building had appeared at Crewe Street which was to be the answer to the problems of Shrewsbury's masons—if not for another century! It was a late Regency style church dedicated to St Michael. To this day the panel announcing the start of this local Anglican church is retained in the Masonic Hall. It reads:

This Church
was erected in the Year 1829 it contains sittings for
810 persons and in consequence of a Grant from
The Incorporated Society for promoting the enlargement
Building and Repairing of Churches and Chapels
630 of that number are hereby declared to be Free
and unappropriated for Ever
W. G. Rowland. Minister

| Joseph Birch, Thomas Lunt | Church |
| John Eddowes, Henry Alfred Floyd | Wardens |

The church was constructed by a well-known local builder called John Carline, and the chancel was added in 1873. The tower, which is a most distinguishing feature, is hexagonal, and 70 feet high. The body of the church when finished was 70 ft 6 in long and 40 ft 6 in wide. The roof is supported by cast iron columns and the ceiling with its squared effect was to prove very fitting for its much later use by the brethren. The church when finished cost little more than £2,000.

We left off our history of Salopian at the point where strict economy was essential and some non-masonic furniture had to be sold for paying off bills. Something of this stringency was to persist for a considerable time and always the desire and dream of local and more permanent residence was maintained. In 1881 we again read of a Committee being appointed to make enquiries about such a possibility in the town, and later in that decade the same effort was resumed. By now the division of the two Provinces of Shropshire and North Wales had been accomplished and it was all the more a reproach to the brethren at the heart of the more compact Province in England that they could not meet in a place wholly dedicated to their business.

Morover, it must never be forgotten that another lodge of almost equal antiquity in Shrewsbury was no less interested in such a development. The Salopian Lodge of Charity obtained its warrant in 1810 from a defunct Antients lodge founded in 1768 in the 13th Regiment. At first this other town lodge was attached to the Regiment of Shropshire Militia but it altered its warrant to a civil one and took its present name in 1820 having settled down in the town when the Regiment was disbanded after the battle of Waterloo. Here then was another pressure for local residence and it is good to note that when eventually the opportunity for a venture actually occurred this lodge was party to the scheme.

During the years that followed three new lodges came on the Shrewsbury scene. They were Pengwerne 3229, Sabrina 4158 and Column 6900. Their arrival and the growth of the numbers of Freemasons only intensified the urge to find a common home and at last under the guidance and with the drive and inspiration of a WBro A. H. Howl, PPJGW and Provincial Grand Secretary of Shropshire, a serious appeal was launched to find the 'missing' hall. The Shrewbury Freemasons Hall Co was set up under his chairmanship and three representatives from the lodges already named were called to form the board. Many buildings were visited in the next few years and inspected for suitability and after very long and protracted negotiations the Church Commissioners at last agreed, in December 1976, to sell the church which was no no longer required. Those who today see its location and the change in population in this part of the town can well understand why at last such a premise would be available now and not previously.

Plans were prepared by WBro W. R. P. Price, the architect, and he was assisted by WBro K. Walton, a Chartered Surveyor. They provided for a lodge temple on the first floor by spanning the space between what had been the church galleries, whilst the seating on the ground floor was removed and a spacious dining room, with kitchen and other facilities, was properly provided. The remarkable thing here is that all this was achieved without in any way altering the appearance of the original church building on the outside. The distinctive church tower serves, as did the pillars of the original temple of Solomon, for storage and a service facility whilst the windows and the placing of the temple floor have been so skilfully dovetailed that you might well think, as you park your car in the ample space provided, you are about to enter a more normal place of worship.

Work commenced in 1978 and was completed in September 1979 but unfortunately, before even the first ceremonies could be held, the chief protagonist for this

The temple on the first floor.

venture, WBro Howl, had been called to the Grand Lodge above. As one enters the present Hall there is another plaque, of more modern vintage, beside the one already referred to. It reads:

To commemorate the establishment of this Freemasons Hall,
   opened in September 1979, and to recognise the courage,
   foresight and initiative over so many years shown by
W.Bro. A.H. Howl, P.S.G.D., Past Dep.Pr.G.M. of Shropshire
   and the professional skill and ability of
W.Bro. W.R.P. Price, P.Pr.J.G.W. Architect and
   W.Bro. K.W. Walton, P.Pr.Gd.Std.B. Quantity Surveyor
In converting St. Michael's Church to the satisfaction
   of the membership.
The foundations were truly laid in the highest traditions
   of the Principles of Ancient Freemasonry.

In regard to the principal character mentioned above and still closely associated with the present membership of the Freemasons Hall Co it is as well to recall the words in the Provincial history of a century ago which said:

...and the Brother, if any, who will in the future be mainly instrumental in procuring its establishment, will lay the Masons of Shrewsbury under an obligation, which no gratitude they can give him will ever discharge.

They were truly prophetic words and it is good indeed to see how much the present beneficiaries of this venture are ready to acknowledge the debt they owe to departed merit.

Moving into this adapted church framework one cannot but be struck by the sense of dignity and care that has attended the workmanship which has been expended on this previously consecrated building. There is not the slightest sense of derogating the previous uses to which it was put (see also Colchester in this volume). Here we have at once a place that welcomes the visitor, makes him at home, and also encourages fellowship. The decorations are recent but tasteful and the effort has been to make the social side of masonry as natural and palatable as possible. Care has been taken about furnishings and lighting, whilst also trying to ensure that as much space as possible can be used.

One mounts the stairs at the old west end and reaches a pleasant landing area where brethren can easily assemble both for lodge or for somewhat larger processions. The woodwork has been chosen with care and the doorway placed so that easy access can be made to what is the lofty upper area of the old church. There can be seen the windows in their old positions, though curtained, and the dais with its uniform set of Master and P.M.s' chairs, each with their pillared backs, having tiny spheres upon them, creates the right atmosphere for what is an older ecclesiastical setting.

During 1980 a special appeal was commenced throughout Shropshire to provide a further memorial to the late A.H. Howl and it was decided that the sum raised would enable new pedestals to be provided and eventually a local craftsman supplied and made a Worshipful Master's, Senior and Junior Wardens' pedestals together with a Secretary's table in matching mahogany suitably inscribed and presented to the Shrewsbury Freemasons' Hall. It is interesting to note that when the emblem was removed from the original W.M.'s pedestal for fitting to the new one the date stamped on it was 1829—the same year as the building of the original church structure.

The many vicissitudes through which the older lodges of the town went, as they moved from place to place, has meant that we do not have here the wealth of early or decorated items that we have mentioned so much elsewhere in these chapters. Yet here, as we said at the start, is one lodge already reaching its bi-centenary and another within sight of the same. Here at last these lodges, each with their incomparable minutes, traditions of working and warrants intact, not to mention their banners, can begin to create a new tradition which their previous members could not boast of—a further century in a place that will properly remind their successors of when their lodge began and be a home of more permanence than any they have hitherto known. Until just before this book was published it was also the masonic home of the late Percy Thrower, beloved of so many gardeners, and a member of Sabrina Lodge from 1949 - 88.

In another, and perhaps less happy, sense this latest hall created from an Anglican church building may become even more memorable because it could be the last, or one of the last, to be created from such a source. When this hall was transferred from its previous owners there was still no serious antipathy to the Craft which undertook to use it for proper purposes. That climate has of late sadly changed, if only, we hope, for a time. It may be some years before this kind of occupation will again be either normal or permissable. It makes the visitor to Shrewsbury's Masonic Hall all the more sensible of that bit of history which it preserves by just being what it is. That it will be carefully and fittingly used by its present owners there can be no doubt.

The master's pedestal and east end.

SPILSBY

The Masonic Hall at the South of the Lincolnshire Wolds

HALFWAY BETWEEN SKEGNESS and Horncastle going west, or between Boston and Louth going north, the traveller will come across the market town of Spilsby. It is not the most visited place in the British Isles and it may at first seem strange that this country place should find its way into the company of such masonic centres as Ludlow and Leicester, Norwich and Nottingham, Boston and Birmingham. What, the reader might well be asking, has Spilsby got that so many of us in much more well-known places apparently lack? The answer is a lodge that is already over 150 years old, a masonic hall full of most unexpected treasures, and, for those who are fortunate enough to be able to attend them, ceremonies that retain features which so many masons have not even realised that they are missing. But first let us go back a little in time.

In March 1932 a medical practitioner, and a member of the lodge here, called Dr F. J. Walker, shared with his brethren the contents of a dream which he claimed to have had. 'I was walking in the streets of Spilsby nearly one hundred years ago when I saw a gentleman come out of a white painted house in High Street and then proceed along it. He met a young man to whom he said, "I do hope things will improve with regard to roads and travelling, now that you have come here, for as you have just left the office of the greatest man on roads (McAdam) we shall look for improvements. It was only last night, when I was driving from a Masonic meeting at Boston on a very cold night, I was held up at the turnpike gates at Toynton. The tollgate keeper was evidently fast asleep and he took nearly an hour to get up, put on his clothes and open the Toll-gates before I could drive on. These gates should be abolished." The young man replied: "I am very sorry, but I am afraid that I cannot order the gates to be kept open during the night, but might suggest, Sir, that you try and raise a Masonic lodge in Spilsby and so save yourself these seventeen miles drive in the cold." The old man thought for a few minutes and then said, "Perhaps you are right and if your suggestion comes to pass I promise that if you wish you shall be the first person to become a member of that lodge".'

'The elder man', said Dr Walker, 'was my great-grandfather, William Walker, one of the founders of the Shakespeare Lodge, and the young man was Thomas Hollis, my grandfather on my mother's side—the first candidate to be initiated

Opposite: *The master's pedestal and chair. The east window shows various masonic symbols and just to the left can be seen the lantern with 'eye' aperture.*

into the same Spilsby Lodge.'

It was indeed when the Provincial Grand Lodge of Lincolnshire met at the Spilsby Town Hall on 11 June, 1835, under the presidency of no less a masonic 'notable' than the famous Rev Dr Oliver, Deputy P. G. M. that the Shakespeare Lodge was dedicated in masonic form and the W M, Major Edward Brackenbury, and the J W, The Rev G. Coltman, also made rapid advancement for they were later that day made Prov S G W and Prov Chaplain respectively. Not only so, but the new Prov Chaplain preached at the Church Service which was customary on those occasions.

The name of the new Lodge may itself cause a few queries to arise in the mind of the reader. How does a lodge in the countryside of south-east Lincolnshire come to bear a name which may seem so improbable. The answer is, of course, that just as the time of its formation was a period when warrants of erased lodges were transferred from their previous owners to new title-holders so also the 'name' could on occasions be so transferred. Moreover, in the case of this lodge it was really rather important to take the name of the earlier lodge because the brethren at Spilsby were inheriting their furniture. As we shall soon see the name of Shakespeare was to be firmly and unforgettably associated with this somewhat remote country temple.

The original Shakespeare Lodge No 516 met, not surprisingly, at the 'White Lion Inn, Stratford upon Avon', having been warranted in 1793. It sadly only lasted for 6 years, and the furniture then went to St John's Lodge No 583, meeting at Henley in Arden—a still quite fitting location. What is more the St John's Lodge very swiftly changed their name also to 'Shakespeare' and remained so as it then began to perambulate, like so many lodges of the period, from tavern to tavern in the Birmingham area. By 1818 it had arrived at the 'White Horse Inn' (no less) in Steelhouse Lane where a Mr Machin was the proprietor. By 1832 the lodge was re-numbered but was obviously ceasing to meet for by the end of 1834 Mr Machin, on moving to a new hotel in Union Street, was wanting to dispose of the unused Shakespeare lodge furniture and it was bought by a Bro Sandars who was then the Governor of Spilsby Prison. He was to be the fourth person mentioned on the warrant of the new Spilsby lodge and how he came to know about the available furniture is easily explained. He came from Alcester in Warwickshire and could easily have heard locally about the available items. He bought it all for £15.

For the first 50 years the lodge met in the old Town Hall of Spilsby but they celebrated their Jubilee by moving to a masonic hall created from a disused Congregational Chapel. In 1910 this was sold and after three years in the Sessions Hall they were able to occupy the present premises—a purpose-built centre which was dedicated on 29 November 1913. In 1922 the brethren bought it from its builder, WBro J. J. Rainey, as a memorial to those brethren of the lodge who had given their lives in the First World War. The mention of Bro Rainey serves to underline for readers the constant lines of family members that have belonged to and served this lodge, which is now the 5th oldest in the Province. We saw how Bro Walker's relatives had been in the lodge at its inception. Bro Rainey too was the fourth in line from his great-grandfather, whilst he was initiated as a Lewis (i.e. at 18 years of age) and was, on his installation, the fourth to carry the family name in that office. A record not yet surpassed. There is also the Dodds family 'connection'.

On approaching the Masonic Hall it seems by no means out of the ordinary. Soundly built of red and cream brick it has a fine gable-end façade with five round-arched windows in the upper storey with the centre one taller than the rest, and four below with the main door between. In the apex of the gable is a circle of brickwork with the words 'Spilsby Masonic Hall' on the stone within, but even this inscription is placed so that only the interested and perceptive visitor would notice it.

Within we find first the essentials of such a local masonic 'home'—cloakroom facilities, a dining room to serve some 50 persons, a workable kitchen area and a straight staircase of normal design at the rear leading to the essential and distinctive ceremonial area above. The benefit of these service rooms was soon felt. In 1915 the masons lent the lower room of the Hall as a recreation room for the wounded soldiers who were undergoing treatment in the drill hall next door. The room, lighting, heating and stationery were provided free until the end of that conflict. In 1940 it was the same. Permission was given to Mrs Wright to use the lower room on Tuesdays of each week for the entertaining of wives of members of HM forces stationed in Spilsby. The soldiers whom we shall meet upstairs doubtless smiled! The fact that there is still little below to distinguish this as a memorable masonic hall must surely reflect the fact, so easily forgotten, that this lodge, like so many others elsewhere, had for so much of its history to occupy a single room for its practices and that even such a room in which its possessions could not be permanently displayed. The furniture, or what is here normally described as the 'lodge regalia', had to be confined to this area and its array was strictly limited. That is certainly still the case here though, of course, the lodge possessions are now largely on view for the permitted visitor all the time.

On entering the temple upstairs one is immediately struck by the stained glass leaded window which occupies the space above the east window drapes, and in the arch of the centre window we noticed outside. It was restored to its Victorian-style freshness by Bros Johnson and Wright and is certainly an immediate reminder of what it is that we enter this room to share in. The window is circular with a scroll-patterned framing also in glass, and at its centre is another smaller circle with a huge open eye set within a 'glory' (a pattern of irradiating lines). From this circle project out eight formal leaves in the shape of ellipses and these point to eight more cloud-like forms in which masonic emblems are displayed. . . the pentagram, the square and Euclid proposition of a Past Master's jewel, a large sprig of acacia, the square and compasses of a WM, a cornucopia under opened compasses, a triangular level, a dove in flight with the olive branch and a more formal 'level' such as appears on a PM's apron. It must, in itself, have been a great day when the masons of this lodge could contemplate having such an adornment to their temple that could remain permanently 'in situ'!

One's eye is immediately drawn then to the first item of the magnificent furniture in the east. The Master's pedestal is of mahogany and about five feet high with a picture painted on copper and let into the front panel. It represents the poet Shakespeare leaning against a column and pointing to the working tools on the floor around him. One should specially notice the presence of the ladder in the bottom right hand corner.

The Master's chair behind the pedestal is gilded and spacious, with a square top formed by having two angular projections on the otherwise gently rounded back

The front of the master's pedestal with a painting representing William Shakespeare pointing out the working tools.

of the chair, that has gilded ears of corn running around the backrest of padded red plush. These corner projections carry small representations of the sun with a face at its centre. Over the centre of the back are fixed Prince of Wales feathers pointing out that the furniture's original lodge was chartered during the Grand Mastership of the Prince of Wales in 1793. The chair also has finely carved arm rests, with claw projections and no less slender grooved and petal-decorated legs.

Immediately in front of the pedestal are two wooden steps. Perched on the two ends of the upper one, so that they appear to be attached to and flank the pedestal, are two wooden columns in the shape of Corinthian pillars with capitals of brass. They are each set upon a base with the letters J and B. It is interesting to note that as the candidate faces the pedestal the J is on the left and the B therefore on the right. This is because, correctly, the pillars are placed as if looking *out of* the temple and hence the pillars are the reverse way for the Master who sits doing just that.

Above the brass capitals are yet two more square blocks of wood which carry, on all their four sides, small tracing boards beautifully worked in fine silver wire and covered with dome-shaped glass covers about 2" in diameter. In the illustration (found in the Transactions of Quatuor Coronati Lodge) the reader will see the detailed and exquisite pictures that are here on view. It will repay any mason to spend time examining these drawings and making himself acquainted with the meaning of each and every one of the symbols there depicted.

Nor is this all. From the top of each block suspends a pattern of hanging fine brass wire in the shape of pomegranates, whilst above even this feature are two globes representing the terrestrial and celestial universes. On the lower of the two steps is a kneeling pad, for it is here, between the two great pillars, that the new mason enters into the solemnities of his truly masonic 'temple'.

The Wardens' chairs fit the Master's. They too are plush seated with gilt, rounded backs, arms and legs and the whole back rest is an oval. The candlesticks behind them were, like the Master's again, designed to fit into the whole pattern of the original lodge and hence are large, grooved pillar-like creations. It is worth noting here that in 1855, when a gas service had just been introduced to Spilsby, the lodge formally decided that they would continue to conduct their activities by candlelight as hitherto.

Yet this is not the end of the immediately distinctive lay-out of the lodge. As one stands by the entrance at the west end it is clear that squaring the lodge here is a necessity. As in the days when the implements would once have been drawn on the floor of an inn so here we see the retention, with actual objects, of that principle. At the north and south-east corners of the flooring are laid the rough and smooth ashlars respectively with the 24 in gauge between them. Then, moving down the centre of the floor, from east to west, you will notice a gavel, a chisel, a square (with one side longer than the other), a level, a plumbrule, a skirret, pencil, compasses and a trowel. It is particularly significant that whilst there are tracing boards (given by an initiate in 1854) the main features for instruction are thus always made visible and the presence of the trowel is not neglected in this now venerable lodge. A tripod with pulley and smooth ashlar completes the line.

The Bible still used on the Master's pedestal has the intriguing inscription 'Shakespeare Lodge Stratford on Avon No 416' even though the proper number should have been 516. What is no less intriguing is the fact that in this lodge the passages used for the various degrees, and at which the VSL is opened, are strikingly different to those used in most lodges that carry on this ancient practice. For the first degree the passage from 2 *Chronicles* 4/5 to 6/13 or 1 *Kings* 8/44 to 10/12 is chosen and this refers to aspects of Solomon's creation of the temple furniture and its use for the Almighty, but not as in the familiar passages elsewhere. The square usually set on the VSL is an ivory one.

For the second degree we note *Isaiah* 9/11 to 22/11 or *Isaiah* 9/17 to 13/8 where the emphasis is on the impending doom for the people of Israel in the face of the coming Assyrian invader; whilst in the third degree the reading is from *Zechariah* 1/1 to 3/9 or from *Ezekiel* 14/17 to 16/51 where we have the preparation for the restoring of the Temple that has been destroyed. For those who know something of the Royal Arch these singular choices of passage have a most remarkable appositeness as the preparation for what should follow the Craft steps, and it is really most instructive to learn that a separate Royal Arch chapter for this lodge was only considered in May 1947. Could it be that the lodge retained readings from its predecessor-owner of the Bible when that lodge would naturally have had a chapter working under its lodge warrant? It is a matter for consideration.

The sword still used by the Inner Guard, and not, it should be noticed, a poignard, is of blue steel and also shows on its blade the head and shoulders of the poet, a triangle with the No 492 and above that a circlet with the words 'Shakespeare Lodge'. These all appear towards the tip of what then becomes in mild fashion a 'wavy sword' such as can be more clearly seen at King's Lynn or Alnwick. On the rest of the blade are sixteen masonic emblems. This was no doubt purchased when the Shakespeare Lodge furniture was used at the Talbot Inn at Henley-in-Arden where, in 1792, the St John's lodge number had been changed to 492 and its name altered then to fit these items.

Indeed the history of this lodge, as dictated by its furniture, is shown by the lovely brass square which lies in that array on the lodge floor. It has the number 531 stamped upon it and this tells us that it was added to the collection about 1814 when the lodge was meeting at the Shakespeare Tavern in New Street, Birmingham.

On the wall of the lodge room are two more pieces of this amazing collection which puzzle both members and guests. They are wooden, outline figures of eighteenth-century soldiers, about five feet in height and with no apparent link with the Craft. I would venture to suggest that they are linked with the members of the first lodge of this name, for certainly the soldier illustrated has a characteristic Warwickshire wheel on the cap badge that he displays. I would dare to presume that they were timely reminders of the first lodge's origins in an army setting and that might account the better for the lodge's demise when those who joined to form it were largely either suddenly dispersed by the call of duty or killed in the Napoleonic Wars that were just beginning to gain momentum when this lodge was founded.

I would be all the more certain if we fully understood what the Secretary of the Spilsby lodge meant when, at its outset and in thanking Sandars for obtaining this 'regalia', he spoke of it 'belonging to the highly appointed Shakespeare Lodge at Stratford on Avon'. Was it that he knew through Sandars of the report in the *Freemasons Magazine* of 4 June, 1793, when the dedication of that first lodge was reported. That certainly seems like the description of an occasion in which county and military folk would be pleased to mingle but where nobility would even be willing to attend.

The description of a Free Ball on that occasion and a song that accompanied it have a distinctly 'uniform' flavour.

One brother wore a suit of Buttons with Masonic emblems &c elegantly set, which cost upwards of Ten Guineas and many wore Aprons worth from Five to Ten pounds each . . . Bro J. Bisset, of St. Albans Lodge, Birmingham, wrote the customary song:

> 'Great Shakspere's name the Pile shall boast
> A name so much renown'd, Sir;
> With flowing Bumpers let this Toast
> The cheerfully go round, Sir.'

It is this atmosphere of urban elegance and show that is still brought here by the

A view of the temple at Spilsby. The two outline figures in the south and north east corners are made of wood and provide a soure of puzzlement to members and visitors.

furniture amongst which we stand and it is doubly sad that the present lodge does not have more than a copy of the original warrant that was granted to the Shakspere Lodge at Warwick.

Yet anyone who imagines that this is the sum total of Spilsby's treasures is mistaken. The lodge still has a piece of the flooring of the 'Holy Temple at Jerusalem' given by the Rev Canon Coltman whom we met earlier and who was the first Junior Warden. The lodge possesses an interesting specimen of a masonic apron. It is wider at the top than at the bottom and there was almost certainly a border which has been cut off. Could this perhaps be one of the aprons of an earlier lodge using the furniture and leaving this amongst the debris? There is also a pewter plate, presented in December 1858, by Mr H. Hobson, a plumber locally, and it is generally assumed to be the same plate still used at the north-east corner for an initiate.

Nor was the lodge niggardly about the benefit which it had from this 'foreign' furniture. It was lent on the occasion of the founding of Horncastle Lodge in March 1870, and their working tools were used in the laying of the foundation stone of the local Wesleyan Chapel.

Yet we cannot leave this fascinating hall without considering for a moment the matter of banners. The one that came with the furniture from Birmingham must have been a fair size, for a minute of 4 February, 1836, states that in setting out the furniture the banner was to be suspended across the western end of the then Lodge room to protect the Senior Warden's back in cold weather. One knows the feeling! What happened to that item we do not know but in 1841 the present banner was purchased. It was designed by one of the Founders and made by a Mr Aukland of 136, The Strand, London, for 4 guineas. On 24 August the lodge had a letter saying that the banner had been sent by van and it was hoped that it arrived soon and safely. It seems to have met neither of these criteria for it is on December 23rd that a minute states that the banner, now arrived, was spoilt in travelling because it was rolled up before the paint was dry. Appeals to the maker must have proved useless for in the next September the Lodge pays 6s 6 d for cleaning the banner and painting a Union Jack upon it! In 1855 it was noticed that it had a Royal Arch border which was 'not in order in a Craft Lodge'. It was altered at a cost of 10 shillings.

It is now, sadly, time to leave this truly memorable Hall. There is no chance here to speak of the unusual third degree ceremony that draws visitors from all around so that seating is at its maximum: or the fact that the lodge does demonstrations of their distinctive Installation ceremony for neighbouring Installed Masters' lodges. Here is a gem of older masonry with remarkable links to the past and the rest of the country set in a small market town in one of England's largest counties. If you visit it you may be sure of this; the meeting day will be the nearest to the full moon so that you can get home with some assurance of being able to find the way; and the date of Installation has been changed—it was St John the Baptist Day in June but in 1844 they decided to make it St John the Evangelist, 27 December. There may be snow, but at least there will be no toll houses!

STAMFORD

The Masonic Hall in a School House

IT WAS 10 MAY 1803 that three members of Lodge No 867 of the Irish Constitution, together with four others from elsewhere, lodged a petition to found the first Antients lodge in the county of Northamptonshire. The name they took, that of Good Intent, may indeed have represented the feelings of those who began the lodge at the Salutation Inn in the Beast Market but it was not to last more than 15 years altogether and in that time its meeting place suggested an endangered species for its name was altered to the 'Stag and Pheasant'. In the 1970s the pleasant old house, with its quoined and keystoned doorway, at last ceased to be an inn and it is now one of Stamford's dentists' surgeries. Yet, as Bro R. J. Linnell has indicated in his fascinating history of freemasonry in the town, we can well imagine those early freemasons passing in and out of that door for we know their names, their occupations, the clothing they wore at that period and even the individual handwriting of some of them. As befits a place with the rich history of Stamford, masonry has a fairly long and recognisable past.

The actual erasure of the Lodge of Good Intent did not in fact take effect until 1827 and it was about this time that the local Bluecoat School, which had been founded as long ago as 1704, moved to a 'room near St Peter's Hill'. It was to remain there for about 13 years and was then replaced by the schoolhouse that forms the present Masonic Hall, situated in All Saints Street. It was then (in 1838) that the Trustees of Charities in Stamford: ... contracted with Mr James Richardson to build a new Bluecoat school-room on the site of the garden adjacent to the late station-house on St Peter's Hill at an expense of £252.

> The building will afford excellent accommodation for 200 scholars; and from the improved rental of the estates and management of the trust, it is expected that nearly that number of boys will be educated, and 80 of them clothed annually ...

That was written in May and in June there were odious comparisons drawn between the excellence of the teaching under the mastership of the Bluecoat school and that of the Grammar school where the Headmaster received an incomparably larger salary. In September the local paper reported:

> The building (situated in a retired passage on St. Peter's Hill) is greatly admired by all who have visited it, both for its style of architecture and its completeness; and it is only to be regretted that it stands on a spot where it is so little seen ... it is designed for the comfortable accommodation of 150 boys ... and will thus be rendered a real blessing to the population of the town.

The reference here to a more restricted number of boys than previously has never been explained but in either case it suggests that the premises were once rather larger than when the freemasons came to occupy them. Moreover, it is strange to read of the school, for all its excellence, being in 'a retired passage'. Those who know it today look upon its yard and frontage through a fine, bold stone archway with two very appropriate stone pillars with central moulding and carved chapiters. A substantial iron-wrought gateway also adorns the entrance. The difference is explained by realising that this gateway was not erected until 1862, a quarter of a century after this building was formally opened. The present owners must be very grateful for this development, and in such a form.

Though there does not seem to have been any local lodge working at this precise time in Stamford there is evidence that the Craft was far from forgotten. The new school-room was in All Saints Street and in the churchyard of All Saints, and close to the sidewalk, there still stands a well-carved masonic gravestone. It bore the inscription, 'Sacred to the memory of William Baker who died 22 June 1838 aged 39 years'. He was obviously not old enough to have joined the Lodge of Good Intent before it ceased to be active and it is therefore a matter for speculation where he practised the Craft. Was it at Peterborough of which we have elsewhere made mention or Northampton where the Pomfret Lodge was warranted in 1819? We shall probably never know (though the subject would make an intriguing local masonic study) and yet, here in the town centre the many schoolboys of the Bluecoat school nearby would be able to see the gleaming symbols honourably borne by one who now lay with his secrets hidden for ever.

It was in Northampton, at an inaugural meeting on 24 June, 1840, and at the Peacock Inn, that the newly warranted Lodge of Merit made its first appearance. In a style with which readers are already familiar it moved rapidly from the Peacock to the Angel (1841), to the Ram in 1845, and even to another town, Oundle, in 1855. In the very year that the gates of the Bluecoat school were erected the Lodge of Merit was at the Dolphin Hotel and was about to have a new number which it has carried ever since—466. A new number may have caused another itch for in 1865 it had found its home here in Stamford Baron at the George Hotel and within ten years it was holding its own Chapter—called the Montagu.

The George Hotel stands in the Northamptonshire part of the town, that is, south of the River Welland, and it is for this reason, despite its present location to the north of that stream that the Lodge of Merit is still part of the Northamptonshire Province. As it is 60 or more years since the lodge left the ancient hostelry and much alteration has taken place in the meanwhile on that site, it is not exactly clear as to which parts of the old inn were used by the Merit brethren. However, during 1984 some further modifications exposed very interesting evidence of the occupation by the masonic lodge, including the following:

(i) the remains of the extensive painted ceiling decorations, which took the form of continuous line-patterns interspersed by groups of squares, compasses, trowels, hexalphas and suns. There was even one part of a seven foot diameter design in the centre of the ceiling which almost certainly displayed a central 'G'.

(ii) There was a huge painted first degree Tracing Board which filled a recess 7 ft 6 in wide with two 9 in returns making a total width of nine feet. The height when fully exposed was 6 ft 6 in but a further 1 ft 4 in at the top was hidden behind a modern pipe casing so the total size was about nine feet wide and over seven feet high. This was at the west end of the temple (for the Entered Apprentice?) and it now seems likely that there would originally have been corresponding second and third degree 'Boards' of similar dimensions on the south and west walls respectively. Whether these have already been destroyed or have yet to come to light we cannot guess but in terms of showing that not all Victorian Tracing Boards were of the moveable or more modest size that we expect these are certainly unusual samples. What is particularly striking, even in the newspaper photograph of the discovery, is the sense of space and perspective that the mural displays. It has about it the same impression that one more normally receives today in a Chapter floorcloth (see the Watling Street Lodge at Stony Stratford).

During these years of its life at the George the lodge's eventual home underwent certain changes in name—from the Bluecoat (Elementary) School, to the Stamford Endowed School to the Endowed (Elementary) School and back to the Bluecoat School. All that by 1927. It was just before that year (in 1924) that the long debated subject of the lodge's tenancy was brought to a head by the receipt of a

The entrance to Stamford Masonic hall with the old school behind.

notice to quit in six months' time. Though it meant moving into the Lincolnshire side of the town the lodge chose the Stamford Hotel as their next venue and moves were immediately made to have the necessary arrangements and modifications made for their removal there. A new lodge room and ante-room were to be fashioned in the existing part of a tall ballroom and the result was what many described as a 'delightful temple'. It had a barrel-vaulted ceiling, pilasters and moulding were preserved and the effect was of unusual intimacy and pleasing detail. The construction was mainly in Ketton stone but also partly in Roach Abbey stone from Yorkshire. 'The front displayed several three-quarter columns of the Corinthian Order supporting an entablature and parapet, and the whole was surmounted by a large statue of Justice, seated, formed in artificial stone. To approach the temple the brethren ascended a winding staircase of impressive proportions and, all in all, the premises provided much food for thought for the discerning mason. For 47 years this was to be the home of the Lodge of Merit, and a very happy and satisfying home it was too'. (J. Linnell, p105)

The first meeting was on 16 March 1925 and the lease was for 21 years. It was for a lot longer period that the Lodge of Merit conducted its affairs here but at last the time came for the brethren to find new premises, a far from easy assignment. 'As a temporary stage in what was to be a long process Merit moved to the old school rooms in Austin Street.' It was to be a 'temporary' resting place for four years! Meanwhile the Bluecoat school had moved to further new premises in Green Lane and the old school house was occupied by the Malcolm Sargent School, named after the well-known conductor who had been a former pupil of the Bluecoat and Stamford Schools and whose father, Henry Edward Sargent, was at one time a Serving Brother and Tyler of the Lodge of Merit. By 1974 this school also moved on and the old school premises were at last vacant.

It is worth noting that at this period there was still a close association of the town authorities and freemasonry. Representatives from the lodge were invited to accompany the Mayor Elect in civic processions and the Worshipful Master and Secretary usually obliged. In particular the lodge was well represented in the official commemoration of 'One Thousand Years of Stamford's Recorded History' and the brethren's appearance on that occasion only served to underline the long association of freemasonry with this ancient town.

In 1972 the lodge suffered the loss of a remarkable 'character'—Brother E. Sisson Dalton, who had been Junior Warden in 1925. Initiated in the Royal Navy he was a member here for 54 years and those who are shown the splendid set of six dozen '466' firing glasses in the upstairs gallery of the present hall will have for ever seen the best reminder of this remarkable man. He was one who might well have enjoyed the move in 1976 to the old school hall and dining room where his gift could be well and truly used. The move was not altogether easy for there had to be sufficient financial support for the venture and that was a heavy load on the resources of but one local lodge. The efforts were successful, however, and on 20 September, 1976, we have the minutes of the meeting held for the first time in permanent premises in Stamford, the property of the Stamford Masonic Centre Co Ltd, ie all Masonic Orders using the building. It added a nice touch to the proceedings to have a greeting read out from WBro L. J. Thoday of St Mary Balham Lodge No 3661 in London, 'Expressing delight at the use of the school as a masonic centre since he had been a pupil at the Bluecoat in the early 1900s and

The east view of the temple with the Lodge of Merit banner and the two globes of particular interest.

was a contemporary of Sir Malcolm Sargent.' (Linnell, p121)

It is also pleasing to the author to record that it was one of the Trustees that was named in that take-over of the school, Bro Fahie, who helped him to see more fully the contents and possessions of the Lodge of Merit. The total outlay was some £20,000 including the cost of the building and the installation of central heating. In a manner not always appreciated by more fortunate masons it was now a complete novelty for the brethren of Stamford not to have to go out for the dining session and to be able to control their own bar and catering. Whereas in many other halls this side of the premises is to be taken for granted we have here a memorable development in itself that when leaving their labours the brethren have but a step to take down a short corridor to their adequate and increasingly well appointed 'place of refreshment'.

We have already mentioned the distinctive gateway to the present Hall—a feature that adorns both the present banner and badge of the lodge—but it is worth adding that until they were erected here these features 'formed an end bay of a six-bay arcaded market front to the Browne's Hospital in which Stukeley had held sway and aroused so much feeling 130 years before. The market had been designed in 1839 by the Rev Henry de Foe Baker of Greetham—the village, incidentally, where one of Stukeley's literary clubs held its monthly meetings. In 1859 this market was replaced by the building opposite, and in 1862 the old one on

The unusual ballot and charity boxes.

the front of the hospital was dismantled. The architect who carried out the work of removal and re-design was Edward Browning who became a joining member of Merit three years later and was its WM in 1872. If anyone notices a similarity between this gate and the façade of the United Reformed Chapel in Star Lane they must not be surprised for their pillars came from the same old market arcade.

One enters the present Hall through a blue door and a perfect church-porch style entrance. On the roof ridge to the right above there once hung the school bell from 1872 but as you turn to the right inside to enter the dining room you will see another interior church belfry type frame with its bell re-hung, still bearing the inscription—'Made by J. Warner & Sons'. It weighs about two-thirds of a hundredweight. The timber was donated largely by the late WBro Scholes who was also a former pupil of the school and a Past Master of several Stamford Lodges. It is still rung to summon brethren to the table.

From the dining room we pass by a small and rather narrow passageway to what can only be described as the 'backstage' arrangements of the temple. Here, in what is still a fairly confined space and surrounded by boxes, a steep stairway of open wooden treads to an upper gallery, and the wooden pillars that support that gallery the Tyler seeks to prepare his candidates and satisfy himself that the latecomers are 'regular'. It is an arrangement that may not continue for much longer for after twelve years of accepting this plan the Trustees are about to propose some modest but useful rearrangements of this section of the building. The west wall of the temple itself is but the partition that rises to the right of this narrow space and the lodge have it in mind to give themselves more space by bringing the west wall back across this area to the real wall on the left, to build a larger and wider corridor between here and the dining room, and to provide a more intimate arrangement for preparing the candidate.

Yet though the present arrangement is not ideal it is good to see for it reminds one of the building's original purpose and lay-out and in this tightly compressed area you can still find not only the firing glasses already mentioned, but a unique chapter pedestal with a top showing the sun, moon and stars; some ancient chapter banner shields in metal; a distinctive chapter floor cloth; and the old Tyler's sword. All is not as meaningless as it may at first appear.

Yet it is inside the temple proper that one would need to go. Here there is at once a sense of age and antiquity which only the combination of the Lodge of Merit's furniture *and* the school hall could provide. The room is lofty and narrow and has a sort of austere fadedness which Dickens might perhaps have described best. It is also a room of such dimensions that almost at once lends itself to the thought that perhaps this is one present-day Masonic Hall that might naturally lend itself to the old 'Moderns' arrangement that is more normally adopted at our dinner tables— of having the wardens in the south- and north west positions rather than in the south and west as we usually find them. This would enable the lodge which is growing in numbers of members and guests to accommodate many more people and, with the west wall still further withdrawn, to give ample space on the floor for adequate perambulation. As it is there is a real sense of closeness and crowdedness which must be added to when the room is filled with masons. Not that closeness to one's fellows is undesirable. Space for movement, however, adds very much to the aura of our Craft and this room, with its sense of history already present, can afford to experiment.

The most striking feature is undoubtedly the huge Lodge of Merit Banner that almost entirely covers the east wall above the Master's place. The banner is square and hangs from a horizontal pole with tassels protruding from the lower corners. Above a scroll bearing the lodge name and number there fans out a huge chequered pavement on which are placed a rough and smooth ashlar with a cramp inserted in the upper side of each. Between them and leaning against an old globe is an open VSL with a circle, around a square and compasses, on the right hand page. Above the globe is a large burst of light and in the centre of the rays a large gleaming EYE with a very heavy lid. Despite the age of the banner this feature dominates the room and must be, for any newly unveiled candidate a most striking presentation. To the left of the light are the crescent moon and stars, whilst on the right are the square and compasses in the open position.

Below the banner and above the bucket chairs that serve (according to their emblems) the DC, ADC, SD and JD and the past masters is a white panelled ceiling of wood with a huge G placed at its centre. Set off by the darker walls and the mahogany senior officers' chairs and pedestals this ceiling perhaps emphasises what could yet be done to enhance the character and attractiveness of this old meeting place. That its lodge is old is shown by two special possessions that stand on a small organ in the south-west corner. The one is a ballot box of pure white which has a somewhat unusual manner of use and is quite unlike any other such box that I have seen; whilst the black and gold curved alms box speaks in language of quite another age: numbered '687' it reads, 'Subscriptions for the Distressed Freemasons' and then in two compartments made between three pillars we see 'Orphan Boys and Girls School' and 'Aged Freemasons Asylum'. The presence of these items alone must awaken in those attending here an awareness of days long gone—though still present in spirit.

Perhaps as we stand in the centre of the lodge once more and look at the east wall we may perceive two items that have hitherto escaped our attention. Halfway up the wall and on little angled corner shelves are two very old globes on their tripods. Of course we have seen these items in so many postions in other halls and have begun to become accustomed to their presence. Let us remember that for many masons these are already part of a past that they have never known in their own meeting places. To the brethren here they might, perhaps, not be as prominently before their eyes as they might be. If the lodge does gain more space and light and some re-design it would be, I believe, a good move to show these old and precious symbols off to greater advantage. They are memorable reminders of an older masonry. For me they will remain an ever present pointer to the Lodge of Merit as very much part of universal masonry.

The ancient Lodge of Merit banner.

STONY STRATFORD

The Masonic Hall on the Old Watling Street

THE ROMAN ROADS of Britain were, until this last generation, the great arteries of traffic throughout the whole of this island. One of those was Watling Street which still bears its name close to St Paul's Cathedral in London but which spread its later tentacles from Dover and Canterbury to the City, and thence past the Roman camp of Verulanium (now St Albans) and the boundary between Leicestershire and Warwickshire to another ancient Roman camp at Wroxeter on the Severn. It was a long and busy thoroughfare and it was to be named in modern times the A5.

If, on approaching the great new city of Milton Keynes from either north or south, you take the line of the old Watling Street and follow its straight and undeviating line you will come at the south end to the old town of Bletchley and at the northern end to Stony Stratford. The main street of the latter was, until quite recently, the main thoroughfare for main road traffic and it is good that to prevent its destruction further a new A5 passes in a broad sweep to the east leaving the town to pursue its more leisurely ways.

At the south end of the main street a slight diversion to the east will bring you to the residential part of the old town in which St Giles parish room stands. On arriving at the latter you have come to a truly delightful Masonic Hall. To enter and look at it now, as any visitor may do, is to see the results of a very great deal of hard work and devoted attention to detail. Moreover, the Working Party, which has been a feature of this site since the 1950s, 'was not a product of planning or formal organisation—it just evolved'. It is the product of tasks innumerable—like that of one brother painstakingly stencilling black dye in the Lodge carpet, others painting the walls, whilst one couple 'built a mobile bar for the convenience of the brethren called from labour to refreshment. It was not until 1965, following the puchase of the Parish Room, that a Working Party, consisting of members regular and irregular, was unofficially and informally constituted'. The author of those words, WBro Eyles, added this comment—'If this sounds a contradiction in terms it is the way things are apt to get done in Watling Street Lodge'.

Let us however stand back a little from the present achievement of turning this parish hall into a listed building for the use of Freemasonry and see something of how this whole project came about. Our journey back in time will be to just over a century ago when the masonic scene in these parts was almost completely empty and everything had yet to be done to give substance to the Craft in Buckinghamshire.

126

The substantial rafters are the dominant feature together with (below) *the two window designs.*

The Master's pedestal and PMs' chairs.

It is true that as early as 1796 a Provincial Grand Master had been appointed (Sir John Throckmorton, Bart) but he was able to avoid overwork for there were no lodges for him to rule. In 1813 the Etonian Lodge No 284 was founded but in 1825 it moved its meeting place to Windsor and hence became a Berkshire lodge. The eventual situation was that in 1847 the masonic provinces of Berkshire and Buckinghamshire were merged and the Marquis of Downshire became their joint head.

Two years later the Grand Secretary responded to a petition by the brethren of Fidelity Lodge No 652, which met at Towcester, asking that a lodge be erected at Stony Stratford and that it be placed under the PGM of Northamptonshire. Sadly they were informed that where they proposed holding the lodge was in that part of the town that was in Buckinghamshire. The Marquis of Downshire's approval had to be obtained but he proved very elusive and after a lengthy interval the project lapsed. It was not until 1852 that the senior lodge in the same province was consecrated as Buckingham Lodge No 861 and that remained the only lodge in the county for the next nine years.

At last, in 1860, Scientific Lodge No 840 was consecrated at the National School, Stony Stratford, and it was this lodge which was the sponsor, 16 years later, for the Watling Street Lodge No 1639. The actual consecration took place at the Cock Hotel in the High Street on 29 August, 1876. The consecrating officer was the VWBro the Rev J. Studholme Brownrigg, PG Chap and Deputy Provincial Grand Master, and another clergyman, the Rev W. F. Short, PG Chap and a Past Master of Apollo University Lodge, Oxford, was the WM designate. The SW also was a clergyman which seems again appropriate in view of the lodge's eventual home.

It is worth noting, as we have not done hitherto in this volume, that the early minutes of the Watling Street Lodge make clear what was the procedure in the small accommodation that the lodge first occupied. Having been 'closed in due and ancient form . . . the lodge room was cleared of its Masonic furniture and the festive board laid for the banquet.' One is immediately bound to wonder just how much furniture was moved—or even possessed—at this stage and where, in a busy hotel, could it with ease and without undue trouble be stored? Certainly the matter was one that would exercise the members of this lodge, as with so many others that we have noted elsewhere. The presentation, at the fourth meeting, and by a brother who appears to have visited but the once, of a set of third degree emblems to be shown to the candidate, only accentuated the problem.

That the matter of 'operative masonry' was never far from the minds of even the early members of this lodge is shown by a very unusual entry in the minutes for May 1879. The Secretary began the debate in lodge by reporting that there had been an appeal for a subscription towards the restoration of St Alban's Abbey. Not only did the lodge members approve the following forthright resolution but they even asked that it be sent as a memorial to both Grand Lodge and Provincial Grand Lodge. It read:

That this Lodge therefore asserts it to be the sacred duty of all true masons to do their utmost in preventing the artistic records of our departed Brethren from being dishonoured or obliterated by the fatal process of falsification called restoration. That to give a practical effect to the foregoing resolution every

Brother be requested to refrain from subscribing to the restoration of any ancient building or edifice unless he is satisfied that such restoration is to be carried out strictly in accordance with the character of architecture in which such edifice or building was originally erected.

It was some statement, and a bold step for a young lodge to take, but it has been a distinguishing characteristic a century later in guiding those masons who set about making the present Masonic Hall fit the style and nature of its original construction. No record, incidentally, exists of any response from either of the senior bodies approached.

That the lodge already had a satisfactory complement of chairs, pedestals and candles is shown by the request of the new Mark lodge in Stony Stratford that it might pay for the loan of these items in its own meetings. With what seems real generosity the charge levied for their use in four meetings a year was only £1! This kindness was to be acknowledged when in May 1890 the attendance at the Craft lodge was so low that it was agreed that, if the Mark masons were willing, the two sets of brethren should dine together. The fact that many of them were in both orders helped. They were to do it more than once.

By the end of the century the numbers again began to increase and another larger room at the Cock was inspected and approved. Even so the Installation meeting could not be accommodated there and St Paul's College nearby was made the venue. In 1902, when the landlord of the Cock became a lodge member, the Banquet Committee was instructed to arrange with this Bro Clarke to hold future meetings in the 'new rooms of the hotel'. These may have been in the yard at the rear of the building and were later known as the Masonic Rooms. It was quite clear that better and more satisfactory arrangements for meetings were going to be a continuing concern for Watling Street brethren.

This was to be emphasised during and after the year in which Bro J. H. Hooker was the Master. A harmonium had now been purchased, by another clergyman in fact, and in 1905 a careful inventory of lodge furniture was undertaken and it was agreed to purchase certain new items. In the light of what we shall shortly see in the present hall it is worth mentioning what was then added to the lodge's possessions. A new lodge carpet (the one already mentioned as being re-marked in parts), 13 new officers' collars, platforms to raise the principal officers' chairs, a level for the SW's and a plumb for the JW's pedestal. A sum of £14 was set aside to carry out the purchases and a new kneeling-stool was presented as a gift by Bro James Jones.

Some indication of where the brethren were meeting at this time is worth noting so as to appreciate the benefit of the change that was now not too far away. The Masonic Rooms at the Cock had been a Drill Hall during the 1914-1918 war and it will be no surprise to learn therefore that they were a plain brick construction 'with no pretensions whatever to architectural distinction. The Lodge used only the top storey which was approached by a flight of wooden steps. The amenities were, by modern standards, minimal'. The top storey was long and narrow as well as drab and again had to be cleared in order to set the tables for meals. The only well-remembered feature was that some of the banquets served were described as sumptuous.

By 1923 the continual dismantling of the lodge furniture was beginning to take its toll and there was both a resolution to repair the items that could be saved (which actually cost one pound) and another to purchase new Tracing Boards and chairs for the Master and Wardens. All this was done and thus the celebrations of the Jubilee meeting were able to be conducted in a setting of more graciousness and dignity. It was an excellent preparation for the move that was to mark the start of their next fifty years.

In 1928, on 3 May, the lodge was held for the first time and by dispensation in the St Giles Parish Room. Dining was to continue at the Cock but the moving of the furniture to this new location was determined. For an annual rent of £17 the brethren were to have their Craft and Mark meetings (12 in all), the full cost of lighting, heating and storage, as well as the exclusive use of the room on their lodge days. A five-year tenure, but renewable, was entered into by the lodge secretary and the Vicar, and the lodge stayed on as tenants until 1965 when they were offered the chance to purchase the property —which they did.

Before the offer for purchase arrived, however, the brethren had had sufficient cause to realise what it was that they were dealing with. In the *History of Watling Street Lodge* (p68f) we read about the conditions of the Parish Room in winter 1952. 'There was a recurrent problem of heating the Lodge Room and the vagaries of the old-fashioned combustion stove and the whistling draughts in the North at WBro Secretary's table and the cold blasts blowing down the necks of the PMs in the East'. A sum that might even exceed £5 (*sic*) was allowed to deal in some part with these matters! There was also some dissatisfaction with the quality of the meals at the Cock and by 1958 it was moved that attempts be made to accommodate the brethren by feeding them at the Parish Room.

It was now time to consider the negotiation of a longer lease but something much more exciting and also demanding was to become a possibility. An emergency meeting on 2 July, 1964, revealed that with only one condition (that of allowing the use of the lower, or dining, area for possible use on Sundays as a Sunday School) the Vicar was willing to sell the Parish Room to the lodge for a round sum of £1000 plus the cost of recent repairs to the entrance (£185). The property was freehold. After careful discussion the lodge decided to go ahead, and a Parish Room Committee was formed. They worked with expedition and by 15 January, 1965, Watling Street Lodge had its own roof over its head.

The continuous effort and generosity of spirit that has produced the charming lodge room and social areas of today is not easy to describe. Everywhere that the visitor looks is marked with items that show the affection and involvement of scores of masons. The Bible cushion and drapes for each of the Master's and Wardens' pedestals, the latter with their special emblems; a reading desk for the Secretary's table; curtains and necessary upholstery—these are some of the expressions of interest and support for what was to become a memorable masonic home for this lodge coming up to a Centenary.

What strikes the visitor to this modest but highly distinctive masonic hall is the excellent way in which these local brethren have combined (as at Warwick or Colchester) to turn an older and somewhat neglected church premise into a place to be truly proud of. The enormous burden of tackling heating, the care of much timbering and roof area, adequate seating, decoration and lighting so that the final effect is a charming and attractive whole is not something to be lightly overlooked. Moreover this hall is memorable especially because of the fraternal feeling which it has generated in the Thursday night working team of a regular dozen workers who have been coming to 'labour' for over 20 years.

From the moment that you enter the small portico doorway and look around you can see what a change there must have been from the days when the members' wives first tried their hands at making their own meals here for the men. 'The kitchen annexe has been rebuilt, and new equipment installed there. On the Vicarage Road side of the building a robing room and toilet facilities have been added, with a "Wild West" feature in the form of a pair of swing doors . . . Owing to the decrepit state of the walls in the present entrance hall and dining room they all had to be panelled—an immense task greatly enhancing the appearance of the room.' A new bar has been installed to replace the mobile one mentioned earlier, but this also meant the demolition of the main staircase to the lodge room above and hence the construction of a new one.

It is at this point that one remarks on the application of the restoration principle mentioned earlier. 'At the end of the dining room was the tower containing a wooden spiral staircase in a decayed and dangerous condition, and therefore never regularly used. With the generous and invaluable help of WBro Charles Head this wooden staircase was removed and replaced by one made of steel and this has now become the main access to the Lodge Room from the ground floor, reminding one of the traditional winding staircase consisting of three, five, seven or more steps.'

From here we can now step into the other *pièce de résistance* of this building— the upper room or temple itself. The sight is indeed calculated to impress. One passes through a doorway flanked by two enormous gilded pillars made of sheet metal representing 'B and J . . .'. With the globes that each of them carries above their carved and decorated chapiters they reach a height of about 10 feet, which seems in true proportion here, for the roof of this temple has 'scissor beam' trusses like those of many a typical medieval church hall. Along the length of the temple run three rows of transverse beams supporting on the one side (south) a series of trefoil-arched clerestory windows, genuine and original but now covered on the outside, in some of which are drawings in colour of scenes from the New Testament (see illustration). On the opposite side the windows, still in place but covered by plastic sheeting pending restoration, fill the gaps between the trusses. The whole room has a most lofty appearance and yet the pale blue wash of the lower walls and the cream wash between the timbers softens what could otherwise be a most sombre and overpowering chamber.

From the west, where a huge golden coloured curtain falls in folds from under a similar pelmet and is completed below by a richly carved reddish brown panelled lower wall, one looks along a grey and black chequered carpet (made by the Working Party c1981), towards a well-organised east wall with its Master's pedestal and drape (bearing the words, and symbol, Watling Steet Lodge No 1639), two wooden panels at the end of a long, blue hanging curtain, a long cream panel above bearing the same number and the four principal banners of the HRA, with a gallery above that, its screen being crimson and the banners of Watling Street and St Giles lodges hanging upon it.

The Master's chair is not of initial masonic provenance though it has spiral pillars supporting the headpiece and the backrest is of cane with a floral design. The chairs flanking the pedestal here are all uniform, with red plush seats and backs, and are finely carved French 'conference chairs'. The blue upholstered cinema tip-up seats with their freshly gilded partitions are strangely fitting and are also very comfortable. A large metal G hangs from the pitch of the roof over the middle of the carpet whilst below it stands the newest tracing board case that was presented to the lodge by a widow in 1952. There are old PMs' shields on the walls and also the warrants we have mentioned. Should the temple be set out for the Royal Arch ceremony a visitor would be specially struck by a further carpet (made by the Working Party in 1983), which gives a remarkable sense of depth into the vault and there shows a circle of the zodiac around a central pedestal.

This then is the product of much unremitting effort and affection over the last generation. Those who have worked on this Parish Room have succeeded in making for the lodges here an unsurpassed temple of masonry in the new city of Milton Keynes, a temple of which the founders—what they call in Watling Street, 'the Eight Originals'—would be not only full of approval but of amazement as well. One most encouraging feature of this hall is that it is generating a great sense of loyalty and support from those of the future who will have to maintain and care for it from now on. For the visitor who can just turn away from the rushing motorway and climb its winding stair there will be something memorable to retain and a pride that masons can labour so well.

Looking at the west of the temple with the substantial pillars beside the entrance.

Guy's Cliff chapel, Warwick.

WARWICK

The Lodge in Saint Mary Magdalen Chapel, Warwick

IF YOU DRIVE north out of Warwick about one mile towards Kenilworth you will eventually see on your right side a lodge cottage and some locked park gates. Opened only when the present local masons wish to have access for their meetings you are on the point of finding one of the most intriguing and perhaps the oldest site for a masonic hall in our country today. Its name is Guy's Cliff and the story of its past history is certainly a record that would more than exhaust the space we have available in this chapter. All that I shall attempt is a brief summary of the story that is fully told in A. F. Porter's excellent booklet on St Mary Magdalen Chapel there.

Those who visit the site, an experience which I recommend, will doubtless be able to obtain a copy and read the full story with new interest. An open invitation is extended to both masonic and non-masonic visitors for whom a guided tour and entertainment can be arranged.

A local historian, John Rous, writing about 1440 AD, affirms that in 500 AD St Dubritius, a priest who had his church where Warwick Castle now stands, built an Oratory here, and dedicated it to St Mary Magdalen (in the time of the Ancient Britons). Later he moved to Wales, to become the first Bishop of St David's. In 1200, or thereabouts, a larger chapel was built, taking in the statue of Guy, which will be explained later.

The saint was the first and only Bishop of Warwick and that for only a brief duration. What is interesting is that the main church eventually erected in the town of Warwick is also named The Collegiate Church of St Mary.

The chapel may have become more and more neglected but in the sixteenth century Leland writes of the site's 'quietude and beauty' whilst Camden mentions it and Fuller wrote: '... a most delicious place, so that a man in many miles riding cannot meet so much variety as there one furlong does afford ... a steep rock full of caves in the bowels thereof, washed at the bottom by a crystal river, besides many cleere springs, all overshadowed by a stately grove ...' Not a word about the chapel—and yet the chapel was there!

We know this to be the case because a century later the *Lansdowne* MS. at the British Museum records that three historians found it. The text says:

On our way (to Kenilworth) and within a mile of Warwick, we saw an old decayed chapel now prophaned in being made a woodhouse. There we found this (Guy's) statue, full three yards in length and answerable to his armour ...

This was a chapel which has been rebuilt from the ruins of the oratory by Richard Beauchamp, Earl of Warwick, in about 1430 AD. Parts of the chapel are clearly older than others, as witnessed by the different stonework between the 'casual' method at the north end (including the huge statue of Guy) and that of the 'masoned' stone, carefully prepared and dressed, as in the rest of the stucture.

The earliest construction seems to have been carried out about the twelfth century, considering the type of armour depicted in Guy's statue. What is important to note is that whilst Beauchamp had the figure 're-cut' the original coat of arms was left intact and these show the family—not of Warwick but of Arden, a family that descended from Rohund, Saxon Earl of Warwick, whose daughter Felice married Guy.

But who was Guy?

Guy was a heroic figure in the songs of the minstrels of the Middle Ages, and was reputed to have lived and died in the caves here. To repeat the legend of Guy would fill several books. In brief . . . he was reputed to be a giant some 8 ft tall, a fearless champion, who never lost in combat. Though not of noble birth he sought the hand of Felice, daughter of the Earl of Warwick. Told that he must prove himself worthy of her he went to Europe, where he won many tournaments, rescued many damsels, slew many giants, etc. Returning to Warwick he married Felice, but after some time he decided to go on a crusade to the Holy Land to fight the Saracens, returning after some years to England as a penitent and palmer. At this time of the story he was said to be weak and ill, but finding Winchester beseiged by the Danes, he engaged their champion, Colbrand, in single combat, and slew him. Guy then came to these caves to live here as a hermit.

He went most days to the castle gates to beg for food, but in spite of his immense size he was not recognised. After some time he was taken mortally ill, and sent his wedding ring to Felice. She hastened to the cave, but arrived too late. Some versions say that in her grief she threw herself over the cliff, (from Felice's Walk), and that they were buried together in the cave. This was about 970 AD when Guy was 70 years old.

It is to this remarkable site, the haunt of regally-approved hermits, that the visitor to a present day Masonic Hall makes his way. At the end of the long and curving drive you do indeed arrive at the caves, which must have provided a suitable dwelling for the hermits Thomas de Lewes in 1334 or John Bury in 1432. It has been found by the present masonic custodians that these caves are perfectly dry 'and maintain an astonishingly even temperature in all climatic conditions. Guy's Well—an artesian spring—still supplies crystal clear water in abundance and is never known to freeze. To a hermit it would at least have appeared a habitable place' (Porter. p8). For the present masonic occupants of the whole property they provide a series of very useful workshops and storage chambers.

The temple at Warwick with central arch pillar and on the south wall the figure of Guy, a reputed giant some eight feet tall. The Master and Wardens' chairs date from 1802 and are known as the 'Harmony chairs'.

It is, of course, at the church building facing these caves that we finally end our journey and that building owes its more substantial appearance to the favour of King Henry V who came to this spot in 1421 and was so impressed with the beauty of the site that he was determined to found a chantry here with accommodation for two priests. He died, at the age of 34, his dream unfulfilled. It was the reign of Henry VI (1423) before the necessary license was granted to the Earls of Warwick to build. Two altars were provided, with housing accommodation above. For 50 years a holy peace, around the singing of daily Mass, was the experience here, and then came Henry VIII!

All the chantry's possessions were granted to Sir Andrew Flammock, Kt, his heirs and successors, and a substantial Tudor mansion was built on to the existing buildings. Parts of that structure are now again coming to light. In four hundred years the property has passed from hand to hand, including the Hudsons, Beaufoys, Greatheeds and Percys. It was Samuel Greatheed in 1751 who built the Guy's Cliff Mansion that the visitor passes on his way up the drive, (and which also accounts for the old gatehouse on the road) and it was he who restored the chapel once more and added the upper part of the tower that we now see. His son, Bertie, pulled down the chapel ceiling and installed the very pleasant plaster vaulting that has remained. The west and north east windows were also 'opened up'.

In 1891 it was the Percys who succeeded to this family and they lived here until 1939 when the mansion was vacated and became a wartime school for evacuees. Thereafter it was bought by Warwick businessmen who hoped to attract American visitors to the area. The project failed, developers moved in to try and create an 'Elite housing estate' but this was not permitted though they were allowed to partially demolish the mansion. The roof despoiled of its valuable lead, and the whole structure cordoned off with barbed wire as unsafe, is a remaining eyesore on what is otherwise a true relic of ancient English history.

By 1955 the property was back in private hands and in 1974 a group of Coventry Lodges (St George's, St Catherine's, Three Spires, Wyley and Coventrian), who were in need of accommodation at very short notice, rented it and adapted the chapel for use as a masonic temple. This arrangement was formalised by a lease in 1975, and existed until the death of the owner WBro Alwyn Porter in 1981; through his generosity the brethren of the five lodges meeting at Guy's Cliff were able to purchase outright the old house, the Gate House, the chapel and approximately seven acres of land, and in so doing have secured a permanent masonic home. It was then, and since, that the immense and patient labours of countless individuals from those lodges have turned this place into the distinctive, workable and promising masonic centre that you see today. The work has been incessant but at least it is now beginning to show results.

We thus come at last to the object of our visit—the Chapel of St Mary Magdalen, or the Masonic Hall at Guy's Cliff. As can be seen from the illustration we are approaching what looks like the church of many a large estate with its square tower and four sprocketed pinnacles, situated at the end of the house's courtyard. We shall enter by the simple arched doorway to the left of the chapel and find ourselves in a narrow corridor that joins the old chapel or temple on the right with the old living quarters or present dining room on the left. Here, at once, we are in the presence of the brotherhood for there is the attendance register desk, the board for lodge notices, some portraits, symbols and pictures of a masonic nature. What we may also not appreciate is the care and attention that has been given to making this property not only usable but habitable. The rooms are dry, warm, properly lit and suitably furnished. It has all been done by loving and voluntary labour by those who, in the words of the author of the chapel's history, A. F. Porter, have enabled Guy's Cliff 'to take on a new lease of life' and 'avoid the Chapel suffering the same fate as the ruined house'.

By discreet but effective lighting and heating, by installing a modern kitchen and re-roofing the older one, it is now possible to feed up to 100 brethren in a medieval cum modern dining room. Not only so, but at last it has begun to be possible to start opening up the next floor above, to ensure that the ancient timbers are treated and lagged so that space for committee meetings or Lodges of instruction can soon be held where once the priests of this chantry had their domestic quarters. The task of preserving, whilst also re-designing, the style of the attic area has been work demanding much skill and great attention to detail. To climb the ancient treads and stand in this recovered chamber and 'bedroom' is a special experience. It is to be hoped that the succeeding ranks of masons here will truly value the effort put in by their predecessors.

Yet the whole re-roofing of the chapel proper which permitted the entry into the old dwelling area was first necessary before the improvement could be made to the chapel below which is now the temple area. Here the brethren made and put down a new wooden floor over the older marble flags, and laid a beautiful carpet. The area and style of the carpet is fairly normal but the chapel, used as a lodge room, is distinguished by one feature that is found nowhere else in England—there stands a great carved pillar between two of the chapel arches almost in the centre of the floor area. This aside, the chapel, with its ceiling repaired and repainted, with vaulted ribs and wooden candelabra, forms a most intimate and dignified setting for the conduct of our rituals. Some of the old pew boxes that previously existed have been changed into benches or even chairs, and to complete and convey the sense of antiquity, which so accords with the best of freemasonry, the Master and his Wardens occupy the chairs dated 1802, known to masons meeting at Guy's Cliff as the 'Harmony Chairs'. Being beautifully carved and inlaid, they are the property of the Lodge of Harmony No 255, and those brethren, not having their own temple, have most generously loaned them to St George's Lodge at Guy's Cliff. It is of interest to note that these chairs were recovered from a storage cellar in Belgrave Square, London in 1974, where they had been stored for many years.

One of the room's most endearing features is the retention of some of the stained glass that was part of the memorial to the historian John Rous already mentioned. Though it is only in two small areas in the north east and north west corners of the temple it is enough to show how this chapel must have looked, or could look, when they were all in place. In one corner, diagonally opposite the main entrance to this temple, still stands the imposing figure of Guy of Warwick, as though proclaiming with his upraised shield and suggestive stump of raised right sword arm, that this place is still under his care and protection.

Moreover, the building is full of still further possibilities of development. The room beyond this temple has now been opened up for use as a temple annexe and instruction room and the dining facilities are also due to be developed as the area of the old house foundations and ruined walls are further repaired. One hope for the future is that perhaps the old entrance can be reconstructed and the tower door closed. This would give a better entry to the building but also means that the temple area would be more protected and private.

Below the chapel is a series of small 'man-made' rooms which were used in the past for food storage, and even below them, excavated out of solid rock, is an old 'ice house', no doubt extensively used before the days of refrigerators. To the north of the chapel, on the bank of the river is a natural cave in the vertical escarpment, its entrance being above flood level. This is traditionally known as Guy's Cave, his supposed last home (Porter p15). At the rear of the cave it was discovered a century ago that there was a panel of Roman and runic characters covered with lichen. Lady Bertie Percy had it cleaned up and the inscription illustrated. It is thought by experts to date from the tenth century, about Guy's time.

The two passages read:

"Y D	"Y T
CRIST – TU ICNIECTI	CRIST – TU CNIHTE
THIS I – WIHTTH	THIS GEWIHT
Guhthi"	Goda"
(in the Mercian dialect of Anglo-Saxon).	(In the West Saxon dialect)

which can mean: 'Cast Out, O Christ, from thy servant (or knight) this weight (or burden)."

Lichen has once more covered the letters since 1980 but their message is hardly one that the modern servants of the GAOTU could repeat in this Guy's Cliff. Those who have produced this memorable Hall have indeed shouldered their burden manfully. When perhaps they do lay it down with their work completed they will be able to do it with great satisfaction to themselves and advantage to all local and more widespread masonry.

WORKSOP

The Hall in an Eighteenth Century Town House

WALK THROUGH THE gracious, porticoed doorway of the house in Potter Street, Worksop, and you will begin to feel at home at once. The potted plant and net curtain just inside the doorway, a typical 'family' portrait of one of the local worthies on the wall, the chairs and occasional table, the warm red rug upon the hall floor, and ahead of you a delightful rise of stairs with red carpet on white treads, white banister posts and dark brown rail. The whole setting is of a well-kept and much prized 'home'. That is what it is and what it was as the history of the Hall by G. Hind will tell you.

The book by a John Holland first describing this property was published in 1826 and was dedicated to no less a person than 'Bernard-Edward, Duke of Norfolk, Earl Marshall . . . Lord of the Manor of Worksop'. Potter Street was described as having many respectable private houses and among them 'a large house built and inhabited by Henry Dunstan Esq., High Sheriff of the County in 1745 and who, owing to an ambiguity in his will, exposed his estate to a series of litigations, which the good people of Worksop will not soon forget . . .'.

Indeed they would not, for after having incurred legal expenses over the inheritance to the tune of £8000 and at last agreed to share the remainder, the contenders were faced with a third claimant who 'presented himself as Mr Dunstan's heir, and employed his friends to take forcible possession of the mansion in Potter Street. This was resisted by the opposite party and a serious fracas ensued; bruises and broken heads were plentifully dealt, and one man was killed on the spot, when further disturbance was prevented, by the judicious advice of the Duke of Portland who was sent for on the occasion. Locally this encounter was known as 'the Battle for the Buslings', the house having been built in an eight-acre field known as 'Buslings Meadow' . . . It can be seen that the present Hall has had a lively past.

In one of the display cabinets today can be found a copy of the 1806 Insurance entry for this property under George Dunstan, Esq, which describes 'stables, offices and chambers . . . All stone or brick and slated.' Even the 'Fire Mark', which stayed in place outside until 1978 is now carefully kept inside the hall as part of its history.

From about 1838 the building became Doctor Heldermiers' Pestalozzian Institution for Young Gentlemen and was described in an 1849 'Visitors' Hand Book of Worksop as 'one of the best conducted institutions of the kind in the country. The establishment is on a most extensive scale. . .'. It lasted until 1857 when a whole series of different owners began to occupy or lease it. At some time before 1899 the original premises were divided into two, as can be grasped by looking again at the frontage and seeing that the old main portico now leads directly to a window whilst the present entrances are two doors on both sides of this.

Eventually the property was left to a Dr Kemp, a member of Pelham Lodge, and on his death was only briefly occupied by his widow, Beatrice. It was at this point that the pressure on local masons to move from their centre in Newcastle Street led them to consider either this property or Scofton House in Park Street. This latter was a large private house now converted into a Territorial Army Centre. On 23 July, 1947, the limited liability company was formed to purchase 33 Potter Street and the sum of £4000 was agreed with Mrs Kemp. By 1948 a mortgage had been agreed but this was paid off within the year following an appeal to members of the lodges. These included the Pelham and Dukeries Craft lodges, the Pelham Chapter and Bassetlaw Mark Lodge.

It was realised on first occupying it that several alterations would have to be made to adapt the premises to the best uses of the units meeting there. The arrangement of the main temple and dining room on the first floor was agreed from the start though by 1960 it was already obvious that some extension work would be required. The work for this period was mainly carried out by two brethren, Bros Slaney and Newbold, and it is fitting that the electronic organ now installed is dedicated to the first of these men, whilst the oak display cabinets and cupboards were placed at the west end of the temple to mark the outstanding contribution of Bro Newbold. It was only as late as 1979 that the real festivities could take place to mark the completion of those major alterations which have made the hall today the delightful meeting place that it is.

Worksop temple laid out with chapter furnishings.

The pleasure experienced by those using the hall today is not least appreciated by those who know something of the past difficulties borne by the members of Pelham Lodge No 939. After its constitution in 1863 it was first at the Corn Exchange where 'Comforts were lacking, the lodge walls needed colouring, a seat had to be provided for the Tyler and a gas stove in the winter to keep him warm'. The lodge began to acquire some essentials—ivory ballot balls, globes, a bench for the PMs and a banner. But in 1878 they had to quit, and after several short stays— one of them even being in a member's private home—they had at last a somewhat better and more permanent centre in the Newcastle Steet room aready mentioned.

Sadly that room was burnt down in 1911 and amongst the whole of the lodge's furniture and fittings, warrant and much regalia were lost. To the delight of some brethren, who can still recall the restored room with its arched and beautifully decorated ceiling painted as a celestial canopy, the lodge room there did continue for a time. No wonder the dedicating officer at the restoration of the Newcastle room remarked on the grit and determination with which the Pelham brethren had risen from the ashes like the Phoenix of old and found even greater strength and beauty. Could it have been the hidden influence of that Phoenix lodge which briefly rested in Worksop about 1802? When at last they did remove to Potter Street their losses were reflected in a desperately sad little note—'to removal of lodge: only 11s 0d.'

It is to the present Hall that we now move. Before we mount the beckoning stairs from the hall it is as well to turn into the Club Room, a pleasant room on the

A general view of the restored Newcastle room.

left of the hallway and look at some of the treasures that have already been re-amassed by this group of lodges. Here you will find two alcoves turned into displays of lovely glass—thick stemmed goblets with ladders and trowels, the pentagram and keys, squares and compasses engraved upon them; another even more delicate wine glass with a tapering stem showing three classical pillars, a mosaic pavement, a rim of swag, two pens, two keys and two interlaced triangles with G between; and two quite tall octagon based firing glasses with grooved sides and another riot of emblems cut into their panels. The whole are tastefully set off against simple green baize ledges and backcloth and can be gently lit. Whilst in another cabinet there are several dishes and punchbowls, decorated in sepia both without and within, showing items of masonic interest that were prevalent long before the Union of the two Grand Lodges made their disappearance certain. One bowl, probably of Liverpool ware about 1796, has the most detailed scenes—one of them showing two Corinthian pillars holding an arch saying 'Holiness to the Lord' with a triangle just below its apex and rays of light permeating all the area below in which there are three crowns, a mitre, the flaming sword, a banner saying 'Kodesh Lo Adonai' and a baroque-style altar with the VSL open on it: the whole surrounded by a huge sprig of acacia on the left and an equally large frond of olive on the other. It is the sort of item that could give any interested mason many occasions for making a daily advancement in masonic knowledge.

Beyond this sitting room and down a short passage you come to what is a most commodious dining room. Gone are the many days of the past when the lodge met in one room and had to repair to some nearby hostelry for its beer and victuals. Here, in a simple, clear-cut but tastefully decorated hall can sit the largest numbers required for local and Provincial masonic functions as well as the annual meetings of other Orders. When fully laid out the room is a credit to the hosts. It is also the only large dining room in the town and caters for most local social occasions, such as the Bassetlaw cricket league division.

Yet it is up the stairs that an eager masonic visitor will want to go. At the head of the stairs there is a delicately-wrought iron gate. It is still secured in place when non-masonic functions take place below but though it is an effective barrier it is so finely made that it in no way hampers the view of what could also be clearly seen without it. Against the pale blue and white lined wallpaper and in the angle of the stairs there stands a long-faced clock with a magnificent mahogany case in very good repair, and having for its face a mass of intriguing masonic symbols. It was made by John Bailey of Horncastle and its features are worth describing.

The circular time face is set in a square painted panel with the three cardinal virtues of Faith holding a chalice, Hope supporting an anchor and Charity with her children, in three of the corners and the skeleton of Old Father Tyme with his scythe in the fourth. Above this square, and in the semi-circle of the wooden case, there is a scene showing a masonic pavement with a stone altar carried on two carved pillars with a globe above each of them. The all-seeing eye above sheds rays upon the altar and in the sky around there is a glowing sun with a face and a man in the moon with seven stars. Below the sky and on the horizon are two gently sloping hills, casting their shadows on a stretch of water. A most evocative scene.

Yet is is the items that form the hours on the face below that must merit our greatest attention. One o'clock is represented by a single ladder, 5 by the V of a partly-opened rule, and 10 by the X of two pens in saltire. The other hours are shown as a two-edged trowel for 2 o'clock; the square and compasses in the 3rd degree position for 3; the maul of the Mark degree for 4; the skull and crossbones for the '6th hour of the day' (the time of the Crucifixion); the perfect ashlar for 7, the perfect number in a mason's lodge; the dove for 8, being the day it was seen returning by Noah; the Level, or Tau, possibly representing 9, for nine right angles; two tyler's swords in saltire—for him who closes each festive board at the 11th hour? And the full moon is shown by the glorious sun of the Junior Warden's post, but with God's all seeing eye beneath it to ensure that all time is seen as belonging to Him. It is a most intriguing item and one that would by itself make this place memorable. The Worksop Priory lodge, then the youngest of the family here, had a first Master who did a wonderful thing in providing this clock for the hall which they and other lodges inhabit.

   To the left of this timepiece there is a charming window casement draped with red velvet curtains. On the window's ledge when I first visited the hall was that very globe of which an earlier description of Pelham Lodge reminded us. The

A grandfather clock with masonic face reputed to have come from Horncastle Masonic Hall. The clock is situated at the top of the staircase behind the wrought iron gate.

whereabouts of its previously neglected partner have just come to light but this is a Malby's Terrestrial Gobe of the early 1800s and its label tells us that it is designed from the 'most authentic sources'. I can only comment that for the visitor to this hall the total impact from below of the gated stairway, the masonic 'grandfather' and the globe on its oak tripod against the window casing forms a most elegant introdution to the no less tasteful landing and meeting rooms above. As you turn with the stair and see the stretches of red carpet, the white banisters and oak rail, the walls coverd with beautifully arranged pictures of the Past Masters, leading on to the old temple and dressing room with its wall length boards of officers one can only rejoice that Worksop masons have at last found a hall to be proud of. Since my first visit to this Hall I understand that the two globes will be sited together in the main temple.

Turning right from the further short flight of stairs and passing through what was the first temple of this hall we emerge into the present main temple and can only be amazed at its size. Looking again from the outside one can begin to appreciate what an added dimension was provided with the 1960s alterations. Here we have a room that can happily meet all requirements for the present and foreseeable future.

Though not lofty the room is spacious and broad. A magnificent chequered and indented carpet covers the main floor area and what is left uncovered is dressed in royal blue carpeting. The rich brown of the Pelham chairs, which must have seemed a trifle overlarge and heavy previously, here come into their own. They and the fine, well carved pedestals, together with the beautiful matching candleholders, form the lodge and sit well amongst the many other gracefully carved chairs that stand at the east end. What is no less pleasing both at the entrance door, and behind the Master's place, is a doorway casement of pure classical form picked out in white and gold and setting the whole in the right mould.

We cannot overlook also the unusual willow pattern circle decorations that are placed at the centre of the cream wall panels that run down the two north and south sides of the temple. Apart from the colourful badges of the lodges meeting here there are also some exquisite drawings of the main masonic implements and one of these, the trowel, looks indeed as if it is in 3-D. These plaques are also a link with the previous lodge room, for some of the embossed paper designs used there are still kept in the attic here. The lightholders may be modern but their Victorian style casings (see the Hall at Neath) are going to mature with time and are already just the correct fitments for this modern but traditional room. The rich red background to the central G in the ceiling, and above all the varied array of further masonic items in the cases to the west of the room serve to complete an unexpected and memorable temple.

When the present Provincial Grand Master of Nottinghamshire was Provincial Grand Chaplain he came, in 1981, to help consecrate the new Ryton lodge in this very temple. In his oration he spoke as follows:

'These old masons were perfectionists, they were building for God and they were building for eternity. There was never any suggestion of "this will have to do for the present". I would want to echo those words as I think of this new masonic home in Worksop. Here is a place that masons have taken trouble over. Their work is never done but what they have already achieved is memorable and worthwhile.' It is a hall that I for one shall enjoy visiting again.

GREAT YARMOUTH

The Royal Masonic Assembly Rooms on the Promenade

THERE IS NO other Hall in the whole of this series which has, like the one at Great Yarmouth, a sight of the sea. Those in King's Lynn and Boston, Sunderland and Whitby, Weymouth and Brighton are likely to catch a whiff of it from time to time but none of them stands, as does this elegant structure, on the very foreshore of a popular East Anglian port. There is no doubt about its position, for on 13 February 1870 the *Great Yarmouth Independent* reported that 'during a fierce North East gale a fire destroyed the South part of the buildings, comprising two billiard rooms and a gent's reading room, causing damage to the extent of seven or eight hundred pounds'.

First called the Assembly and Dancing Rooms, the hall was built on its own island site, in the year 1863. Albert Square was then part of the Victoria Building Company's Estate and was designed to provide a place where those who both resided and visited the seaside town could amuse themselves with propriety, in reading, relaxing, dancing and no doubt playing cards. The daughter of the resident manager having given the alarm of the outbreak of the fire above mentioned it is hardly surprising to read that after the rooms were restored for use a lease on them was granted to her father, Mr Novis; but on 15 August, 1874, we find them again up for sale and by the 27th they had been disposed of for £5,050.

It was the next owner, Mr W. Butcher, who appears to have leased the premises to the Artilley Militia who then changed the name of the place to 'The Artillery Mess Rooms'. When the regiment became connected with the monarchy they were designated the 'Royal Assembly Rooms' and the epithet 'Royal' was retained when the freemasons finally purchased this hall almost 70 years ago. What is certain is that even before the hall was fully acquired for the Craft there were many connections through military personnel—HRH the Prince of Wales (GM 1874–1901); Lord Suffield (Provincial Grand Master for Norfolk, 1876–98); and Lt Col Raymond F. Boileau (also Provincial Grand Master).

One link that is clearly visible is that of the interesting shields that adorn the walls of the main temple to this day. These were the result of a rule that each officer of the regiment should present one on his appointment and in total there were about 100 of them. Only a few of them are on show today but those that are displayed have real heraldic significance and can provide a serious topic for study by the knowledgeable visitor. What is of masonic interest is that the Provincial Grand Master of Norfolk is the 'Herald' responsible for these shields, which are

The senior warden's pedestal in the foreground is overlooked by the gallery. The shields around the wall can be clearly seen.

allowed to be kept in this hall on the promise of safe custody and adequate insurance.

Freemasonry, of course, had flourished in Yarmouth for a century before there was any formal association between this hall and the brethren of local lodges. There was the Angel Lodge No 96, founded in 1751 and meeting at the Three Tuns, Bridge Street. It ceased in 1831. A Lodge of Unity No 531, was constituted on 7 October, 1793, and had 51 initiates and joining members in less than 2 years! It was a mariners' lodge and amongst its registered members were Norwegians, Danes and Swedes. Another lodge, also called 'Unity', had started at Norwich, migrated to Acle, and then settled in Yarmouth in 1791. It was soon busy making masons but did not persist. A fourth, however, and one that used these present premises prior to their full purchase, was called 'The United Friends of Great Yarmouth' No 313, and began its life in 1797. It was to become a prosperous lodge and by 1813 it had no less then 207 names on its register. It is of this lodge's history that there are abundant examples in the present Assembly Rooms and one of these is worth mentioning right away.

On 12 April, 1799, a glazier, John Cutlove, was initiated into United Friends Lodge, and when, on 21 October, 1805, Lord Nelson died on the Victory, it was apparently decided that the lodge should have a perfect ashlar connecting its own constitution with that historic event. The result is what is today called 'The Nelson Stone'. This is a perfect white stone ashlar with a cramp in the upper surface. On the obverse are the words carved:

> LODGE of United Friends No. 564
> Constituted on Friday 11th August
> A.L. 5797.   A.D. 1797
> (Groove of excision)
> JAMES DAVY Senr. Warden
> WILLm. MADDISON Junr. Warden
> JOHN GREEN Junr. Secretary

Whilst on the reverse is a rather more striking inscription:

> In Memory of Bro^r Ld V^t NELSON
> of the Niles of Burnham Thorp in
> Norfolk who lost his life in the arms
> of Victory in an engagement with
> ye Combin'd Fleets of France & Spain
> of Cape Trafalgar Oct^t 21, 1805
> Proposed by Bro. John Cutlove

Two questions immediately rise to one's mind on seeing this stone. Why was there an excision of what was obviously the name of the first Master, Samuel Fromow, and why is the great Lord Nelson so blatantly described on a masonic stone for use in a private lodge as 'brother'? The answer to both queries seems to be one of complete uncertainty. It is said that there were masonic reasons for excluding the Master's name but there are no facts to corroborate the step—and equally no lodge records have yet been found to show, as some contend, that it was in this Yarmouth lodge that the famous seaman was initiated.

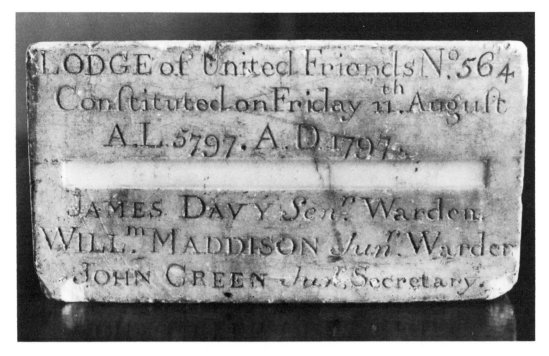

The two sides of the Nelson stone.

Happily it is not our task to solve or pursue such mysteries here. Only to record the intriguing facts of one item in this distinctive Masonic Hall. Another fact is that within a period of 20 years the Lodge of United Friends moved no less than 6 times, but by 1823 was so prosperous that the old Jewish Synagogue in St George's Paved Row West was bought and therafter was known locally as the 'Masonic Hall'. That hall, says the historian of the lodge, 'was a gloomy place, and there appeared to have been no accommodation for refreshment.' At the north end was a gallery of wood with a light iron balcony on which were the appropriate emblems of a Master and his Wardens with their characteristics, WS and B, and the three cardinal virtues—Faith, Hope and Charity. A brass plaque commemorating this move and the dedication of the old hall was previously kept in the Albert Square building, brought here by the Friendship Lodge, to which it was unexpectedly given when United Friendship finally left there in 1840.

It would certainly have been at this period that the lodge was using the set of three oak chairs covered in dark crimson leather which are now prize possessions of the Assembly Rooms. The Senior Warden would also have had his 'hutch'—a large square piece of furniture in place of the usual pedestal. As the illustration shows it was very much more capable of taking a large tripod than is often the case. The lodge had also acquired two antique globes on four-legged supports and these, with the rest of the lights, ashlars and tools must have made any room look distinguished.

Even more so was the 'Anson' chair which seems to belong to the French Imperial period, and though it now carries a square and compasses on the triangular headpiece this was added at a later date. 'Splendidly gilt' and covered with blue velvet lining both inside and out, decorated with sphinxes, lotus flowers, lions' heads and claws, and bearing a superb laurel wreath in gold on the back, this item is one that any hall would be proud to possess, and is by some thought to be

The masonic hall at Great Yarmouth is within sight of the sea.

even more handsome than the one at Norwich which is occupied by the Provincial Grand Masters to this day.

The chair was that in which the Prince of Wales sat when he came to preside at the laying of the first stone of the new masonic temple in Norwich in 1928. Prior to such an occupant it seems to have also been used for the ancient custom of 'chairing' the newly-elected Member of Parliament when the Hon George Anson was in that office. The holes for the carrying poles have disappeared by now but there seems no doubt that it was once so used.

It is not surprising that by 1891 United Friends Lodge was seeking more ample and permanent accommodation. Evidence in the 1880s shows that they were unable to keep their ancient and full-size Tracing Boards (see the halls at Newport, Isle of Wight; York; and Royal Cumberland, Bath) and were at times unable to trace other possessions. When the lodge moved at last as tenants into the Assembly Rooms their first task was to have an examination of the lodge furniture. In the minutes for 12 January 1891 we read of, among other items—three large and three small pedestals, two globes, SW's 'pedestal', three emblems of M., SW's red cloth board and banner. They were at last going to settle down and did so 'in these comfortable quarters' until 1912.

'The meetings were held in the Red Room, decorated with family portraits belonging to Lord Suffield, the Colonel of the regiment *and* the PGM. The installation banquets took place in the large Assembly Room, with its heraldic

achievements'. The balcony in this latter hall was even used for the purpose of having a band, whilst at the tables, from 1896, the brethren were once more able to wield the firing glasses which were at last returned to their rightful home.

During the First Great War the Assembly Rooms were used for housing troops but by 1919 the step was taken of finally acquiring the present premises on a permanent basis. Inside the main corridor of the building there is now a well-maintained brass plaque that commemorates this great occasion. It reads:

This tablet is placed by
the Masonic Brethren of Gt. Yarmouth in
Appreciation of services rendered by
W.Bro. Alfred William Yallop
Master of Lodge Friendship 100. A.L. 5918
Senior Grand Warden of Norfolk. A.L. 5920
under whose zealous leadership
This building was purchased and opened
for the benefit of the Craft A.L. 5919

Much repair was certainly needed and many alterations and improvements were carried out. The south side of the building was extended over what had been a bowls green and thus provided a much needed larger dining room. A card and reading room was retained in accord with the building's original purpose save that now it was not as open to the public. There was also a masonic library and today there are beautifully illuminated cases in the main corridor showing off some of the fine glass and china that the hall contains.

The purchasers of these fine rooms would have been pleased with the results today. The façade facing the sea is decorated in a pale blue and white bringing out the gracious arches that form a projecting arcade and shield the recessed windows of the main hall, which is of majestic proportions. Here we see a long rectangular room, with tall white pilasters dividing the wall into bays of pale blue, save for where two end doors and a central ceremonial entrance take up the white decoration once more. The seating is of uniform mahogany chairs with padded back rests and around the frieze above the heads of the pillars are wreaths of moulding. Above the central doors is the iron balustrade of the balcony which has enabled music to be provided for ladies' evenings or even wedding breakfasts.

Whilst in no way pretentious the visitor to this Masonic Hall cannot but be conscious of a real sense of achievement in having made use of a local landmark and turned it into a very pleasing masonic centre. It has character and style and a history to go with it. The lodges that meet here can truly rejoice that this is a home to be proud of. As you look at the picture of Friendship Lodge celebrating its centenary in the sawdust ring of the Great Yarmouth Hippodrome, or the Provincial Grand Master assisting at the dedication of the organ casing in the largest parish church in England—the one here in Yarmouth—or you note the ancient and preserved banner of United Friends, you can only delight to have seen one more of masonry's treasures in East Anglia. You may get blown away when you go out to get your car but the memory of the Royal Assembly Rooms on Yarmouth's front will stay with you.

INDEX

People and Places

Objects and Symbols